D1287623

Motivation Triggers:

Psychological Tactics for Energy, Willpower, Self-Discipline, and Fast Action

By Patrick King

Social Interaction and Conversation Coach at
www.PatrickKingConsulting.com

Table of Contents

Chapter 1: Understanding Motivation

Quality is not an act, it's a habit

- *Aristotle*

What is motivation?

You've picked up a book about motivation, but let's assume for a second that it's not all that obvious what motivation actually *is*.

Is motivation an emotion or more like a thought? Is it a life philosophy, an attitude, or the way you're born? Could it even be a human need, or a moral code of conduct for living life?

Look at the world and all the things people push themselves to do.

Why write a book?

Why go for a jog this morning (and every morning)?

Why climb the mountain, travel to Turkey, learn Braille, go to therapy, get a degree or take up watercolor painting?

By reading this book, the idea is to hone in on a new way of answering the above questions, especially as they play out in your own life. More than that, you'll be able to use your accumulated understanding and insight into how people are motivated to act toward great things, and apply your new knowledge toward your own goals. Motivation is behind everything we do—it touches on who we are, what we want, what we believe.

Few topics get so quickly to the heart of the human condition, and allow us to look so deeply into *why* we do things (or don't do them!), how we generate curiosity, satisfaction, achievement, and power for ourselves, how we make meaning for our lives, how we set challenging goals and learn the skills needed to achieve them, how we cultivate our creativity, regulate our emotional worlds and take all those millions of single steps that make up the long, long journey to a life that's genuinely awesome.

Motivation is something that's often associated with performance, athletics, sports or perhaps the business environment when people need to be roused to work hard toward financial targets. But mastery of the mechanics of motivation can help us in so many more ways. If it involves thinking, feeling, or behaving/acting in the world, then a good understanding of underlying motivation will add useful insight.

This book differs from some you might have read before: when we study "motivation science" we are trying to marry theoretical understanding with *concrete, practical action*. Changes to behavior and habit. Changes to attitude. Even, in the case of exercise goals, changes to your very physical form.

Anything you Want

If the question is how to attain what you want, then the answer is *probably* motivation.

Let's put it this way: motivation will not make you achieve every grand, glittering goal you can dream up, or catapult you into untold fame, glory and achievement. But on the other hand, no goal—not a single one— was ever achieved *without* motivation.

The focus of this book will be empirical and action-oriented. We call it motivation "science" because it's supported by peer-reviewed research, testable hypotheses and models of human behavior that we can critically assess for their real-world value. In other words, it's about doing what works.

When you hear the word "motivation" you may imagine a cheesy speaker on a stage with too-white teeth telling you to aim for the stars, or bland images of inspirational quotes and people doing fancy yoga poses on Instagram. In this book, however, we'll be holding ourselves accountable to a more rigorous intellectual framework of understanding. We'll adopt *only* those ideas and theories that are well-supported, logically sound and, most important of all, demonstrate real results. We'll also abandon any pet theories that don't stand up to proper scrutiny—no matter how much we like them!

Why does anyone do anything? The answers will be as varied as the people we're talking about. We do things because they're intrinsically enjoyable...

or because we're paid to...

or because we feel it satisfies our needs to...

or because we feel guilty if we don't...

or because we believe doing so will lead us to our goals.

Each of these motivations is drastically different. If we want to boost motivation, we have to have a careful understanding of what motivation really is, and what's driving it.

What is motivation?

Let's start not with an inspirational quote but with some useful definitions to narrow down exactly what we're talking about when we talk about motivation. We can say that **motivation is the collection of psychological forces that allow us to initiate, organize and persist with behaviors that will ultimately lead us to the achievement of a goal.**

Every time you act, whether it's socially, emotionally, biologically or otherwise, something *caused* that action—i.e. something motivated you. Once an action is instigated and planned out, motivation also helps to keep it going, for however long it takes.

Psychologists have dozens of theories to explain why we do what we do. Whether they talk about instincts, or drives, or urges, and whether the motivation comes from inside you (**intrinsic motivation**) or from outside (**extrinsic motivation**), it all comes down to the same thing: something in us desires a change from the current state.

In Johnmarshall Reeve's seminal work on motivation, *Understanding Motivation and Emotion*, this desire for change is a source of energy that riles us up to actively engage with our surrounding environment. It may be taking up exercise, starting a meditation discipline or committing to a daily language lesson, but whatever it is, it's filled with the energized, goal-oriented action that solves problems, thinks creatively, and *gets things done*.

Intrinsic goals come from our needs as individuals—goals can address physiological needs (health, physical mastery, comfort), but also psychological, social or emotional needs (like self-esteem or a sense of meaning and purpose). But of course, we don't exist in a vacuum, and the world we live in also motivates and directs our behavior from the outside.

Most activities, when you think about it, are a blend of both intrinsic and extrinsic motivators—we may act because of our deeply held values and principles, but these themselves may have been heavily impressed on us by our history and our particular environment.

Human beings only act when that action is perceived as meaningful, relevant, correct or beneficial in some way.

And humans arrive at these assessments internally, driven by their own goals, their own needs, and their own values and principles. Though it's true that the external threat of being fired certainly "motivates" people to work hard at their jobs, the decision to actually work hard, the internal justification, is still a personal one.

It follows, then, that motivation doesn't exist where there is no meaning behind the task, no true value, no real relevance to the person involved. Any manager dealing with an uninspired and apathetic workforce knows this—you can't *force* motivation any more than you can force love or interest or care. It has to be genuine.

And this leads us to another aspect of learning about motivation—i.e., how we can influence and understand people around us and the way that they behave. It makes sense that in order to inspire or encourage someone to act in a certain way, you need to acknowledge and align with their own innate, genuine needs, goals and values.

Influence is not the same as force—it's more about appealing to natural forces already underway. You can coerce someone with aggression, but you can never make anyone *want* to do something they don't want to do—otherwise the entire field of advertising would be unnecessary!

The concept is simple: motivation has to come from within. By seeing what motivation is, we also learn what it isn't— the use of force or aggression to control someone or get them to comply. You may have some success treating yourself this way, but any changes to behavior will be short-lived and you'll hate the process the whole way.

A person who is voluntarily and willingly acting according to their own interests... isn't that the same as an overall happy, healthy person?

In other words, what's the difference between motivation and plain old happiness, or inspiration, or some other emotion?

While these are all excellent areas to explore, this book will focus on only a specific set of questions. Let's look at what motivation *isn't*.

"Happiness," contentment, well-being, etc.—the truth is that you could be extremely happy but not particularly motivated to do anything. Likewise, you've probably known yourself to be motivated to act without feeling like rainbows and puppies at that very moment. Though it's usually the case that many positive feelings follow an achievement of a goal, this is best thought of as a *consequence and not a pre-condition.*

Let's look at another obvious one—isn't what motivates most people simply money? Actually, money is more like an incentive than a true motivation (remember, motivation must genuinely address inner needs, values and goals). It's true that in today's world, many activities don't require authentic enthusiasm and deep motivation—to simply be incentivized to do boring admin at work, for example, is enough.

Money is a factor, but it is not *the* factor. Economic necessity cannot replace sincere enthusiasm and desire. Though it's a great stepping-stone and can certainly boost a temporarily flagging drive, it doesn't lead to true satisfaction. Why? Because it's external and superficial, whereas the satisfaction that comes from real motivation is internal and lasting.

What about "inspiration"? How does that differ from motivation? Despite first appearances, they are not interchangeable. Inspiration is fleeting, unpredictable, and largely out of our control. It just strikes us out of the blue one day, and we're usually clueless about its origins. We suddenly feel moved by a touching speech, or energized by some hopeful prospect, and we're so fired up we're buzzing.

But this is not the same as motivation. Why? For the same reason that money isn't—it's purely external and superficial. Inspiration is flimsy. Easy come, easy go. Motivation, on the other hand, builds slowly, day by day, one honored commitment at a time. Motivation is conscious, deliberate and hard-working.

It's the thrilling feeling of reaching down inside yourself and creating something strong and valuable—something to be proud of. Inspiration, on the other hand, is like a flash from the gods, a little flicker of potential. Cool while it happens, but nothing substantial. Inspiration can certainly instigate a deeper motivation, but without patience, focus, hard work and all the rest, it's just feathers on the breeze.

When you look at a motivated person, they seem filled with passion and inspiration. But it's a mistake to assume that this emotional state is the *cause*—really, it's the *effect* of their motivation.

Some managers think of motivation as a "push" factor—something that compels people to act, whether it's punishments, rewards, or incentives—whereas inspiration is a "pull" factor—something that encourages you to reach further, and go beyond yourself.

Many successful authors and creatives will say that inspiration is basically worthless; all that matters at the end of the day is what you *do*. How many words you put on the page. How many reps you do in the gym. How many times you put one foot in front of the other.

Different theorists have different takes on the subtle differences, but there is a place for both the flash of excited vision...and the dedication to sit through the steps required to bring that vision to life. There is a place for firing up your heart and soul, and wanting to act toward some grand masterplan, but it will not amount to anything unless it's also paired with dogged determination and good habits. Head *and* heart. Hope *and* pragmatism.

The perils of believing that either one alone is enough can be seen in a common example: a person sees a friend losing weight and becoming extremely fit, and they feel inspired. What a great idea! They want to do the same thing! With all that passion and energy, they embark on a new goal, and set to work devising an action plan. Within two months the energy has completely fizzled and they're back at square one. Uninspired.

The problem is obvious: pure inspiration is not enough. The reverse situation is the boss who offers plenty of perks and good pay, but asks his employees to do 100 percent meaningless, soul-sucking, and unchallenging work. The problem is also obvious here: not enough inspiration.

We're not teasing apart these subtly different definitions just for fun—instead, when we can see exactly what we mean by "motivation," we give ourselves a clear theoretical starting point, and lay the groundwork for true insight. Inspiration is also *what it feels like* to be motivated, to have a goal, or to imagine achieving it. It's a subjective, experiential state. Motivation, on the other hand, has more to do with our thoughts, behaviors, beliefs, attitudes and ultimately behaviors. It's what we choose from an empowered and conscious state.

Obviously, there is some overlap. Motivation and emotion are strongly connected. Emotions are our conscious experiences, our reactions to events and situations, our inner state of being. But when we remember that achieving our goals often has the side effect of positive emotions, emotions themselves can be a motivator for future behavior. In this way our emotional state and our motivation can reciprocally reinforce one another.

The result of goal achievement, then, is not just the intrinsic value of the goal itself, but also the feelings we derive from that goal, as well as the positive reinforcement to our confidence and self-esteem when we achieve what we say we will.

Science, History, and Biology

Ever since humankind realized we had the ability to consciously choose how to act, we've wondered about our deeper motivations. Philosophical traditions looking into the nature of motivation have considered our **biological** drives and intuitions, the **emotional** and **psychological** reasons for this or that behavior, and the **environmental** causes behind an individual's actions. Some theories attempt to cover all these aspects.

The philosopher Aristotle was fond of the topic, and one of the first to propose a formal breakdown of the (he believed four) different types of motivation. Many of the ancient philosophers were similarly concerned with moral and virtuous action, the good life and what it meant to live properly and to one's fullest human potential.

The idea was to restrain undisciplined, wayward impulses of the heart that would derail you from your chosen, rational goal, and seek a balanced, serene middle path through life. Hard work, patience, humility, rational thought and resilience were seen as key attributes for the well-developed human being, and motivation was essentially the fuel needed to drive that project.

Not all of the Greek philosophers agreed—the Hedonists and to some extent the Epicureans believed that all human beings were motivated toward maximizing pleasure and minimizing pain. Here, "pleasure" could also entail emotional, spiritual or social rewards. According to this belief, to motivate yourself to achieve a goal, all you need do is ensure that the process of achieving actually feels good, in some way—or at least, it feels better than the alternatives (we'll see later on that this original theory has a sound physiological basis).

Later on, many analytical European philosophers ran with various threads of the motivation debate, including the likes of John Locke, Thomas Hobbes, and Jeremy Bentham. Their theories can be boiled down to many of the same ideas we've encountered in this book: people have multiple reasons behind their actions, but it's uniformly our understanding of this cause and effect relationship, and the anticipation of a desired consequence, that drives our behavior.

Queries into motivation have seeped into far-reaching intellectual corners all through history. Freud famously claimed that our motivations are hidden from us in our unconscious mind, and we are all driven by hidden sexual and aggressive instincts that are repressed out of conscious awareness. Freud was responsible for much of the framing of human motivation as a "drive"—i.e. more akin to a biological urge that could be dangerous if not channeled correctly.

Current psychological research is more holistic and a little kinder. Maslow's Hierarchy of Needs, for example, suggested that people were motivated to act according to needs that corresponded to their level of development. Someone with all their material and survival needs met will be motivated to attain other, higher needs, such as those for self-esteem and mastery, or love and belonging with other people. The person who is freaking out about their next meal, however, is naturally going to be motivated by very different incentives.

Similarly, H. A. Murray claimed that there were innate personality differences in what motivates people. People could be motivated to act toward needs of achievement, affiliation (i.e. love and companionship with others), autonomy (independence), dominance (the ability to control self and others), order or understanding (including curiosity and reason).

Other continental philosophers have suggested a more existential slant to understanding human behavior. Humans act, many theorists believed, because they seek to create meaning, to live purpose-driven lives, or to feel and express a sense of control over themselves and the world. In many ways, Darwin's theory of evolution is a complete and comprehensive study of not just human motivation, but the motivation driving all life on earth.

We don't have the time or space to consider the complete history of motivation theories in this book, but hopefully you can agree that the topic is a lot more complex than it appears on the surface. You may be wondering why philosophers and psychologists (and yes, unfortunately, marketers and politicians) have been so obsessed with this aspect of human nature. You may be wondering why *you* should care about it.

The answer goes beyond "you need motivation to achieve your goals."

Think of it this way: you only have finite resources in this life—limited time, energy, money. If you are motivated, you use what resources you have in the best way possible. With a laser-like focus on your goal and a practical, organized way to achieve it, you naturally become more efficient.

Why fritter away the time and energy you have in life to serve other people's agendas or goals? Why waste the one precious life you have on distraction or avoidance?

Knowing exactly how to reach your goals is actually two rewards in one:

a. The reward of achieving the end goal in itself.
b. The reward of knowing you *can* do it, and all the confidence, pride and

satisfaction that comes with this achievement.

People who know how to work with motivation are more productive, more resilient and more solution-oriented. Have you ever seen someone accomplishing impressive feats and wondered, *Wow, how the hell do they do that?*

Well, it's not a superpower. These super-achievers have simply tapped into their own personal source of motivation. You have your own source too—and plugging into it is what this book is all about.

Once you're on a path of motivated, self-disciplined living, you may even start to realize that it's not all that much about the goals anyway. When your entire body, heart and mind are enthusiastically tuned toward the fulfilment of one inspiring goal, it's as though you're fired up and come alive. These are the people who bounce out of bed in the morning, busting with energy.

When you're motivated, things just flow. You may get tired, sure, but somehow it doesn't seem to bring you down. With a strong sense of autonomy and purpose, you start living a life that is richer, fuller and more passionate. You *care* about something—and that's energizing in itself!

When you understand how good it feels to claim your innate right to self-determination, you'll feel happier and more content—not because you anticipate a positive reward for your behavior, but because the path itself has become enjoyable. You enjoy the process of improvement itself, relishing your own growth.

What could be more inspiring than watching yourself achieve the little goals you set for yourself every day? What a wonderful antidote to depression and anxiety—to really know and internalize the fact that change is always possible, and that today can be better than yesterday, even if only incrementally.

This positive attitude will spill over into everything you do, far beyond your chosen goal. A good attitude is infectious, and attracts great people to you. Being positive, motivated and internally driven, you encourage and inspire others, inviting people to respond to you with the same enthusiasm and zeal.

As you develop a more solid work ethic, your self-confidence will deepen, and you'll learn what it means to make a commitment, to others and to yourself. You'll take good care of time and resources, and become more organized—and you may discover that those around you are inspired by your attitude and more willing to help you on your path.

Why does motivation matter? Because your life matters—your dreams, your potential and your desires matter. And the best way to achieve them is with an empowered, focused approach that *takes action*.

This is not just fanciful theory. Successful people the world over, in every walk of life, have found it's motivation and hard work that pays off. There is a famous anecdote about the golfer Gary Player, who was practicing when someone commented, "I'd give anything to hit like that," and Gary replied instantly, "No, you wouldn't."

He then went on to explain what he *had given* already—the endless hours of blood, sweat and tears, the millions of practice strokes, early mornings, bloody bandaged hands... Our culture is obsessed with the genius or the overnight success, the person who hits the jackpot easily and without breaking a sweat. But what Gary Player was saying was clear: he wasn't born Gary Player either. He had to work for it.

Leonardo da Vinci devoted the bulk of every day of his life to painting, and only had his big break at forty-six years old. He painted the whole way, day in, day out. Famous authors like Toni Morrison squeezed in their writing alongside full-time jobs. J. K. Rowling wrote in the evenings and before sunrise. James Joyce is estimated to have spent approximately *eight hours a day, seven days a week* writing *Ulysses*.

Elon Musk doesn't cite any fancy early training in either business or rocket science. He claims he just "started reading books" and followed his own motivation. When footballer Tom Brady told his family he would be a household name one day, they laughed at him. He carried on anyway. He says, "What are you willing to do and what are you willing to give up to be the best you can be? You only have so much energy and the clock ticks on all of us." He wanted to be a footballer, and he gave his life to that end. Pure, complete motivation and dedication.

With motivation, you take a hold of your life and shape it according to your will, your purpose, your passion. You dig deep into the things that really, truly matter to you and take that fire out into the world to build something bigger than yourself. And you do it in tiny, incremental steps, every single day.

This book is intended to help you figure out exactly how to become more motivated in your own life.

We'll be looking at practical, effective techniques to make sure you're acting strategically toward your goals, squeezing the most out of your effort. If you're already feeling motivated, this book will help you boost your enthusiasm to new levels. But if you're struggling to find your own inner power and purpose, this book can help you tackle low motivation and have you feeling inspired to put in the work, today.

At the end of every chapter, we'll condense down the key points to reinforce what we've covered. By the time you finish reading the last page, the hope is that you'll feel spurred to take real, meaningful action in your own life—not just for today, but for the rest of your life.

The Takeaway:

- Motivation is the collection of psychological forces that allow us to **initiate, organize and persist** with behaviors that will ultimately lead us to the achievement of a goal. There are several ways to conceptualize what motivates us, but these can broadly be characterized into intrinsic and extrinsic motivators. Intrinsic motivators derive from our own desires and needs, as we feel an inner desire to accomplish certain goals, while extrinsic motivators come from external sources.

- Motivation is distinct from related concepts like happiness and inspiration. One can be happy but not motivated, and vice versa. The impulse that makes you do something isn't the same as the feeling of euphoria. Similarly, inspiration itself can be a motivator, but while inspiration is short-lived and unpredictable, motivation needs to be cultivated through discipline and action. Inspiration can also be a result of motivation instead of the other way round.

- Throughout history, different people have espoused different reasons and goals behind our motivations, and these have all culminated in the modern understanding of the concept. Aristotle was the first to recognize that motivation results from internal cognitive processes, while those like Locke and Hobbes recognized our desire for a particular consequence as what motivates us. Freud ventured into the subconscious territory of our brain to postulate that hidden sexual desires are behind our motivations. Today, frameworks like Maslow's Hierarchy of Needs dominate our understanding of motivation.

- Though motivation is a complicated concept, the reason it's so important is that we have finite resources for achieving our goals. By harnessing our power for motivation, we can be more resilient, more productive, and more goal-oriented in an effort to get what we want and incorporate the habits we desire. No goal has ever been achieved without motivation, and if you have large, long-term goals, motivating yourself is the only way to pull them off.

Chapter 2: The Science of Motivated Action

Self-knowledge is the great power by which we comprehend and control our lives.

- *Vernon Howard*

Let's begin by getting a firmer grasp of the theory behind motivation. We've briefly considered the older philosophical models that first tried to conceptualize motivation, but from here on, we'll mostly work within a more contemporary, psychological perspective.

There are three main psychological theories explaining motivation. If you've ever read anything on motivation before, it's likely that it touched on at least one of them. A psychologist would agree with the definition we started this book with— **motivation is the collection of psychological forces that allow us to initiate, organize and persist with behaviors that will ultimately lead us to the achievement of a goal.**

Because there are different types of need (for example, psychological or physiological), some theories focus more heavily on one than the other. Humans are messy, though (or should we say "complex"?), and our behavior is likely caused by *many* different driving forces, both intrinsic and extrinsic, that address a range of needs. Therefore the three theories we'll look at shortly are not competing, but complementary.

How do we put it all together? Our needs, the surrounding environment, thoughts, emotions, desires and behavior...? This is where we need a simple model.

Let's consider an example. Your friend invites you to a yoga class and while there, you really enjoy yourself. The class has an effect on you—your stress levels drop, your body fills with endorphins and you feel socially connected to your friend. Since you have a need to feel good and socialize positively with others, your perception of the various benefits comes together to create a desire to want to act to sustain this feeling, or get more of it. This alters your behavior, and you sign up for more classes.

This example sums up the general motivation process. Antecedent (pre-existing) conditions in our environment can have effects on our emotions, thoughts and needs. We interpret these and build an urge for more (or for less, if we want to avoid a painful condition). We are then energized and directed to act toward our goal. It's simple: environmental stimuli can shape our motives, which express themselves in goal-directed action.

When it comes down to it, there's a big difference between *can* and *will*—and that difference is motivation. You can have all the right conditions set and all the competencies needed, but you won't achieve anything unless you are motivated to do so. Without that crucial middle step—the one where you generate the urge to move toward or away from something—you remain stuck in inaction.

We can either be pulled by the promise of the future or pushed by the past, but one way or another, effort is required. Crucially, we all experience **motives**, but not all of us set **goals** (or achieve them). If you haven't eaten in a while your hunger is certainly a strong physiological motive, but it isn't fulfilled until you make a concrete plan about how to act—i.e., you have a goal (get your hands on a sandwich urgently). Motivation is what allows us to cross the divide between *could* and *did*, between *potential* and *actual*.

Generally, the motives, urges and desires that serve to sustain life (food, water, shelter and yes, sex) are push motivators. We drink water to avoid dying of dehydration, pay our taxes to avoid going to jail, or wear a sweater to avoid getting cold. Those things in life that would be nice to have but aren't strictly necessary are often pull motivators. We delay gratification, devote ourselves to a discipline and work ultra-hard for these more abstract rewards of pride, achievement, satisfaction, and even the less noble but no less motivating force of simply wanting to boast or be better than someone else!

What about a person who decides to embark on training to become a doctor, for example? What's motivating them?

It could be push factors to sate more physiological needs (doctors earn boatloads of money and always have job security) as well as pull factors (such as wanting to impress others, to personally overcome the challenge, to serve the community, or simply get nagging family members off your back). Such a person could be driven by a whole cocktail of motives (feelings and thoughts about what being a doctor means) as well as incentives (the hefty salary, respect and admiration from others) and even the desire to avoid unpleasant outcomes (such as, uh, disappointing a mother who wants you to be a doctor).

We can understand our final *resulting actions as the outcome of a mix of interacting causes*—internal and external, push and pull, positive and negative, physical, social, psychological or even spiritual. The way we act is the sum of these influences.

Three Primary Theories

Let's dive into the theories. Though some ideas on motivation seem complicated on the surface, most of them boil down to one of the following themes:

Instinct theory

"I act because I have an inbuilt, fixed impulse to do so. These behaviors evolved because they help me to satisfy my basic needs and survive in the world."

Examples:

Someone acts in self-defense to protect themselves from a dangerous intruder.

A bird migrates to a warmer climate.

Instinct theory was at its heyday in the 1920s but is now largely relegated to evolutionary and genetic research rather than complex human behavior.

Drives and needs theory

"I act in order to meet my various needs."

Example: Someone chooses a big meal at a restaurant after not eating all day.

It's also been hypothesized that people act to reduce the inner tension created from an unmet drive. These don't necessarily have to be drives for survival—for example, a person may have a strong drive to eat a big meal even though they've scoffed three big meals already that day! The biological motivation is there, yet it's uncoupled from survival.

Arousal theory

"I act to maintain an optimal state of arousal for me, personally."

Examples:

Someone goes to a theme park with friends to alleviate boredom and do something exciting.

Another person comes home from a hectic day at work and immediately has a hot bath and a glass of wine to wind down.

Most of the reasons why we do things can be explained using one or all of these theories. Why work? To earn money. Money helps with survival (instinct theory) but also satisfies other needs (such as self-esteem and pride). We might work to avoid the pain of unemployment, while also working to enjoy the pleasure of being appreciated, praised and recognized.

We could have chosen our line of employment because it suits our energy levels and temperament well (arousal theory). We could stay in our jobs because we strive to be excellent, accomplished (or even more altruistic) people—but we also put up with the daily drudgery that comes with that job out of guilt.

Whether we desire power, fame, financial reward, personal passion, philanthropy or personal development, our deeper motivations for any behavior are likely to be explained very basically by one or more of the above theories.

Let's take a closer look.

Instinct Theory

As we saw above, instinct theory suggests that, as biological organisms, humans have innate drives to behave in ways that increase their chances of survival. Think about the instinct of, say, running in terror from something seriously scary. This is something that you do spontaneously and automatically, without being taught, and it can certainly be thought of as goal-oriented (the goal: don't die!).

Furthermore, instincts are broad patterns of behavior: *every* animal in a species shows the same instinctual patterns. All dogs shake when wet. All babies show a suckling instinct and all mothers show an urge to care for their offspring, regardless of their historical period or culture (or how impossible their child is being…).

In other words, your desire for food, water, sex, or safety is not much different from another animal's desire to lay its eggs on the beach or migrate south when it gets cold. Even the tiniest human infants show instincts to move toward the breast to suckle, or grasp tightly onto an offered finger.

William McDougall was the original instinct theorist when it came to motivation, and claimed that three things made up an instinct: perception, behavior and emotion. Other prominent theorists wrote about the power of instincts to drive behavior, including Freud, who theorized that there were only two main ones: the life instinct (everything life-affirming such as sex, food and social behavior) and the death instinct (aggression and the impulse to self-destruct). The psychologist William James identified several instinctual emotions, which themselves occur universally in humans without learning, and are there for our survival (think of instincts to hygiene, anger at a violation, shame or even love).

From this viewpoint, instincts are biological imperatives. They serve a real, practical purpose. Organisms act simply because their instincts tell them to. It's in their genes. Though the idea makes some sense, you can probably see why these theories largely fell out of favor some decades ago: they don't explain *all* human behavior—not even close. Instincts are hard to measure or observe, and even if we identify an instinct, there are still times when the instinct actually isn't displayed.

On the flipside, this theory doesn't explain how we manage to do things that go against our instincts. These include activities that are tedious, boring, dangerous and generally tasks that we avoid but recognize the need for. This could be studying extensively before a test, completing difficult tasks that seem intimidating, etc. It's hard to believe that any natural instinct could be behind our motivation to do any of these things.

Moreover, even if we could attribute some instinct for every behavior, this doesn't tell us anything about why or how these instincts motivate us. As such, this theory leaves no way for us to motivate ourselves. We're stuck waiting for our natural instincts to motivate us through processes that we have no deeper understanding of.

The modern, more humanistic approach to motivation is that although biological instincts play a role, more complex and sophisticated behaviors also come down to our conscious human response to events, and our individual differences. While this model may help us understand more "basic" behaviors, it's less useful to explain why someone would, for example, seek out dangerous situations, develop anorexia or adopt a child.

By the definitions given above, so much of human behavior simply *isn't* universal. Some mothers kill their children. Some people commit suicide. If you try to list right now the behaviors that *all* human beings worldwide engage in automatically almost all of the time, you'd be left with a very small percentage of total human behavior.

Nevertheless, instinct theory is not useless. Some theorists claim that in humans, the instinctual impulse is universal, but its *expression* can be changed according to environmental forces such as culture. The world modern human beings live in is a far less physical, animalistic reality—though humans might have started out as primarily instinctual beings, most would agree that we've evolved significantly more convoluted motivations since.

Drives and Needs Theory

As our understanding of what human beings really want expanded, so did our theories to explain their motivation. If it's not just instincts, then what else exactly is compelling people to act as they do? Ask a mother why she had a child and she probably won't say, "My biology compelled me." More likely is that she will talk about love, of the journey of motherhood, of her psychological, familial, cultural and even financial, political and spiritual reasons behind her decision.

The idea of a psychological need expands the human repertoire to more than just running from saber-toothed creatures and prowling for a mate. While you would certainly die without food, water or shelter, isn't it also true that you need love, purpose, creative expression, meaningful work and so on to be happy and healthy as a human being?

Psychological needs are many and multilayered, and can vary somewhat between individuals. Human beings need to feel achievement at something in life, to feel autonomous and independent to make their own unique decisions, to have somewhere they belong socially, to have a sense of order and control over themselves and the environment around them, and to be able to ask questions so they can learn and understand the world they live in.

Some of the current trends have pushed these psychological needs further—don't human beings also have higher needs? The so-called existential needs speak to our yearning for purpose and meaning, for a rich, self-determined life, and a satisfactory answer to the question of who we are and what we're doing here.

Maslow's famous Hierarchy of Needs theory seems to explain how humans are indeed motivated to fulfill *all* of these needs— including physical, psychological and emotional/spiritual. His idea, though, was that not all needs were the same; i.e., there is a hierarchy. Maslow's theory can be envisioned as a pyramid with the most urgent and necessary needs forming the base, and the less urgent, more abstract needs resting on top.

Our most primal, basic motivations are (necessarily) geared toward satisfying those needs that form the basis of our survival. These important needs come before any others—simply because nothing else can be considered if you're starving, freezing to death, or under threat of immediate attack, for example. This means that the higher needs—i.e. for love and belonging, self-esteem and recognition, and finally full self-actualization, in that order— are not met until the supporting needs are sufficiently satisfied.

Physiological needs: food, water, warmth, sleep, sex, shelter from the elements

Safety needs: enough money, physical and personal safety, good health and well-being

Social needs: feeling love and belonging, friendship, intimacy

Self-esteem needs: respect, achievement, social recognition, a sense of contribution, status, attention, prestige, self-respect, independence, confidence

Self-actualization: realizing full human potential, unique striving for meaning and purpose, state of conscious development and growth. To be "actualized" is to make your full potential a reality, whether it's to be a great parent, businessman, artist, athlete, philanthropist, etc.

For Maslow, all levels below self-actualization come from "deprivation"—i.e., they are overcome in order to avoid the unpleasantness of not having them fulfilled. The final level, however, is a growth need (or what others may call a pull factor) that comes from an inner desire not simply to avoid pain, but to be a better human being.

Maslow believed only 2 percent of the population ever achieve self-actualization, but their characteristics included acceptance of self and others, spontaneity, humor, an objective and neutral attitude to reality, creativity, solution-focused instead of self-focused, unique, altruistic, appreciative of life, ethical, private and fair-minded (to be fair, Maslow only based this on the traits of his personal favorite handful of white, wealthy Western men).

Whether you agree with the needs listed or their order, or even with the claim that one cannot tackle higher needs without lower ones being met first, there is still plenty to be gained from this theory. For instance, what kind of needs dominate your life currently? Do you need to satisfy some more immediate concerns before you can achieve loftier goals?

Again, our needs and drives interact with one another to produce final behavior. If your external incentives and challenges strongly compel you to do something, you'll probably do it even if your internal motivation is weak. Similarly, you will likely act even if external incentives are lacking if your inner drive is strong.

If both inner and outer forces are weak, though, there's simply no reason to act. As people move up the hierarchy, they may find themselves engaging less and less with external incentives, force, necessity and physiological urge, and motivated more by the desire to grow, to develop, connect, and aspire to higher ideals.

As we move up the pyramid, time scales change, too. Physiological needs tend to be immediate and short term, whereas higher goals concern longer time periods. We can further understand Maslow's hierarchy in terms of classifying needs as either traits or states. A need can be a temporary state of being (e.g. you're hungry right now, so you need to eat) or a trait or fixed characteristic (e.g. you generally need a fixed amount of food every day, over your lifetime).

What all this theoretical complexity comes down to is simple: needs and drives of all kinds are powerful motivators, and inform much of our behavior. The many strands explored in this theoretical framework prove how multifaceted humans themselves are. You may have a personality that predisposes you to a high need for independence and autonomy, but you didn't exactly have this attribute as a three-year-old, and you mostly feel this way at work or with friends, and not with romantic partners.

You may have many high-minded goals for yourself that include doing charity work, creating meaningful art or contemplating the universe in general, but it all goes out the window if your blood sugar's low or you're a few weeks behind on rent and the landlady is knocking at the door. You may have strong sexual physiological needs that you nevertheless routinely suppress because of the family and culture you were raised in.

You may dislike your work most days, but still do it because you're quite partial to the hefty salary you get. You may not be bothered to make lunch if you're only a little peckish, but if the intensity of that hunger goes up, you'll eventually cave... unless you're also being nagged by hungry kids who want to eat *now*, in which case you could be persuaded to act sooner...

The drives theory is thus at odds with, yet very similar to the instincts theory. The latter claims that we are motivated by universal drives, that we desire to manifest something we feel instinctively inclined toward. The drive theory, on the other hand, says that we're motivated by a desire to neutralize the drives we experience. When we feel hungry, instinct theory says that we eat because the sensation of hunger gives rise to an instinct for food. The drives theory would claim that we eat because we want to get rid of the sensation (or drive) of hunger. It's a subtle difference, but one motivation is positive, while the other is negative in nature. However, in both cases, we're being motivated by need and impulses that we don't control.

The point of the drives theory is, we're all unique, and biological, social, emotional, psychological, and self-actualizing needs exist in a complex environment with constantly changing incentives, limits, cultures, and people with *their* own respective needs and behaviors. However complex we make the theory about human drives and needs, one thing remains the same: *our final behavior will always be the sum of the total forces—internal and external, push and pull, from all levels—that act on us.*

Arousal Theory

Let's consider one more prominent theoretical thread—the role of individual arousal in motivation. This theory states that people act in order to maintain the perfect level of arousal *for themselves*, and what is optimal differs from person to person. "Arousal" here basically refers to the overall physiological level of stimulation we experience, which affects the way we process information, how stressed or overwhelmed we feel, and how well we perform.

The idea is that humans do what they do to try to balance out their energy and arousal levels. If you're bored and feeling down, you might do something exciting or stimulating like go out to a club or have a run. If you're fed up, overwhelmed, or have had "too much" you might compensate by taking a nap, or spending quiet time alone with a book.

It doesn't really matter what actions or activities we do, only that we perceive them as having an effect on our stimulation levels, and act accordingly to keep ourselves in a healthy equilibrium. One person's exhilarating activity could be another's relaxing afternoon, or someone might love high-energy antics—but only up to a specific point, at which they become draining.

The main idea is that all behavior comes down to the management of a total, single quantity called physiological arousal. Why does someone write a book, commit a crime, choose the burger and not the salad, take up Jiu Jitsu or bail on a friend's birthday party? This theory's answer is that, in some way, these actions brought the people doing them into a more comfortable level of arousal, whether by spiking their arousal or calming it down.

Rather than acting to reduce the tension that comes with mounting unfulfilled drives (i.e. the drive-reduction theory of motivation), this theory suggests that action is corrective and maintains overall homeostasis. The ideal arousal level varies not just between people, but within individuals, and can be shifted by environmental factors, life experience or just the mood you're in that day.

One important aspect of this theory is its claims about performance. Increasing arousal levels generally increases performance, but only up to a point, beyond which they inhibit performance—this is called the Yerkes-Dodson Law, which was defined in the early 1900s. What's more, high-level tasks are more sensitive to optimal arousal conditions than more mundane tasks—you can do simple tasks well even half-asleep, for example.

If you've ever written an exam, you already understand this phenomenon—stress a little and you're alert and focused, stress too much and you start to forget things and make mistakes. Again, however, what counts as the ideal amount of arousal varies between individuals. And the ideal arousal level for each activity differs—you need a whole lot more arousal just before you step into the boxing ring than you do before you perform delicate brain surgery.

Naturally, many variables other than the nature and complexity of a task affect this relationship, including how skilled you are ordinarily at the task, your overall personality (are you very anxious generally?), or your confidence levels.

What does this theory mean for those wanting to improve their own motivation? If arousal (i.e. motivation) is too low, your efforts should be focused on raising it— inspiring action, practicing self-discipline, improving self-esteem and training. If you're overly anxious, however, your approach should actually be to bring arousal down. The counterintuitive result is that less pressure may actually make such people perform better in the long run.

This is a perfect illustration of why we need to understand the theory behind motivation before attempting to optimize it. By digging into the deeper mechanisms of our own motivation, we can understand ourselves and our behavior better, and give ourselves the chance to make effective changes that actually work for us. This is the aim of the next section.

Theories into Application and Practice

We've covered a lot of theoretical ground in this chapter, but now is the time to see just how all these ideas can be put to practical use. The following section boils it all down to three actionable steps you can take right now to enhance your own behavior, performance and satisfaction in life. Each of these steps comes from the three broad theories we've discussed above.

Working with in-built instinct (following your intuition)

You've heard of "trusting your gut."

It's that visceral, inexplicable feeling that makes you feel like you "just know" what you're meant to do. Whether in love, work or money, respecting our innate instinctual feelings can pay off. But there's nothing mystical about any of it. Instinct is nothing more than the ability to rapidly perceive cues and patterns and act spontaneously without any deliberate or conscious realization that you are doing so—and it's a phenomenon that's been researched by everyone from economists to microbiologists.

How can we use in-built instinct to become better people?

This fast, emotional decision-making style is so prominent because it helps humans survive. In fact, many theorists from Kahneman and Tversky to Malcolm Gladwell believe most of our decisions are made this way. The idea that emotions cloud decision making may be backwards—it could be that rational thought and justification follows long after we've already decided what we want to do. Though intuition certainly helps, it can also hinder, and many of humankind's worst biases come in when we follow automatic assumptions without further reflection.

Biases can include believing that we have all the information needed to make a decision, ignoring information that doesn't support the beliefs we already have (confirmation bias), believing we had better knowledge in the past than we really did (hindsight bias), or putting more weight into recent events than more distant ones.

The secret may be to combine both reason and intuition—you can certainly listen to your gut, but it doesn't have to be a one-way conversation! Don't take your own judgments at face value. Really slow down to analyze the facts in front of you, objectively and comprehensively. Intuition is the unconscious appraisal of information—and it's often right. But using it together with your slower, more rational mind gives you the best chance of making a decision that will have the optimal outcome.

Start with intuition and go from there. Put into words your vague feelings, and look closely at them. "I just know we're meant to be together" could open the way for understanding that you're simply experiencing strong physical chemistry, for example. When you dig deeper and give yourself the chance to tally up previously ignored information, you might come to the decision that eloping to Vegas with the person you just met is probably not the smartest idea—even if your gut is telling you to!

The trouble with labeling an impulse a "gut feeling" or "instinct" (in the lay sense) is that it doesn't really explain or mean much—it's just a description, and a weak one at that. Your gut can be wrong, plain and simple, and you won't know it's wrong unless you examine it more closely. Your instinctive mind is a valuable asset, but so too is your rational, slower and more analytical thought process.

If you're trying to make a decision, immediately ask your gut first. Ask trusted others too—the "group gut" is more powerful than we give it credit for—before you make a decision. Then, ask yourself whether your instinct is rational. So if you feel that you're "meant to be" with someone, consider whether there are any actual indicators of compatibility and ensure you're not just assuming this based on your feelings. Think it over, but don't spend too long overanalyzing. A good-enough decision is often better than wasting time chewing over things endlessly.

Match your caution to the size of the decision—if it's something small, reversible and largely inconsequential, you'll probably gain more in experience by simply acting, even if you're a little unsure.

Practically speaking, here's a decision-making checklist to cover all your bases:

1. Have I paid attention to the information and what my gut is saying, or am I rushing to a conclusion because I'm anxious?
2. Am I using my "gut" as an excuse to not examine my real motivations?
3. Will my gut feeling change if I engage my rational mind?
4. Is my gut feeling really just fear or the opinions or others?
5. Do I actually have enough data to make this decision?

Once you've done a more thorough analysis, you can ask your gut a second time. If all else fails, "sleep on it" is excellent advice. This is especially useful when you have to make decisions while you're in a heightened emotional state, like when you're angry or upset. In such scenarios your rationality can easily become distorted, and delaying the decision gives you space to assess your options. Trust your unconscious mind to work on the problem and look at things afresh in the morning.

Working with compassion—know your needs and the needs of others

An easy way to be more compassionate and understanding is to begin with a consideration of human need. Using a needs model like Maslow's hierarchy, for example, we can approach ourselves and others with a respect for the level of need they're operating from. A CEO might understand that he cannot expect high-level, innovative solutions from his employees if he they're constantly worried for their financial security—or worse, work in an environment that undermines their safety.

Similarly, a teacher can communicate differently with students if he can tell that one has a high need for affiliation and approval while the other strongly desires autonomy and control. In relationships, we can be kind with our partners when we realize they may be acting from unmet needs—and we can work to help get them met, rather than being frustrated with their behavior.

It's true that many have disagreed with Maslow's rankings, claiming for example that many materially impoverished families nevertheless do not feel unfulfilled socially, lack self-esteem, or ignore the higher artistic, spiritual or philanthropic pursuits. Similarly, many people have almost all their needs met early on in life and never go on to achieve self-actualization.

Nevertheless, the hierarchy can help us prioritize needs, whether we're understanding our own behavior or trying to appeal to others. When you realize that you're underperforming because you have a vitamin deficiency or are sleep deprived, you open the door to practice self-compassion and self-care—plus you improve your performance.

Many people feel profoundly unfulfilled and empty in life, despite having enormous material wealth and safety. By understanding that their more advanced needs aren't being met, they can redirect their attention to where they are truly unfulfilled, for example by reaching out to others socially, choosing a more challenging career or project, or seeking spiritual or personal growth.

When you frame behaviors in terms of needs, you are tackling things directly. You can ask yourself routinely, *What needs are unfulfilled at the moment? How can I satisfy them?* When dealing with others, you can ask the same question, quickly dissolving misunderstanding and conflict and getting to the root of the problem—i.e. that people behave as they do because they are trying to get their needs met.

Understanding needs can even lead to more creative problem solving. If you are experiencing a lack in one area, you can lean more heavily into another temporarily, for example drawing on friends and family or even tapping into your religious beliefs to help you get though a health challenge or financial setback.

Maslow strongly believed that it was no use studying pathology and mental illness— rather, we could learn more about mankind's full potential by studying those most fully developed people. In the same way, you can look aspirationally ahead to the needs you have yet to fill, and be inspired and motivated to go beyond yourself and realize your full potential.

These theories work very well in the workplace. If you're managing or leading people, ask what their needs are, and how they're going about meeting them—this will help you communicate with them better, as well as incentivize them most effectively. This tactic also works in social relationships of all kinds—remember, it's not what you perceive to be the person's need, but what they perceive it to be. It's the *felt* experience, and not any "objective" reality, that determines a person's perspective and behavior.

In both work and personal life, Maslow's theory teaches us that nobody is a robot. We are all multifaceted beings with all kinds of needs, and a harsh workplace culture that doesn't consider its employees' range of needs will likely alienate or distress them.

When you're making a decision or tackling a problem, ask the following questions:

- Running through all my needs, what am I missing?
- Are my needs being met in my relationships, my career, my community and so on?
- Am I doing enough to understand the needs of those around me?
- What action can I take right now to start addressing my most pressing need?
- What really matters to me, not just immediately, but in general?
- What would self-actualization look like for me?
- What unmet needs are holding me back from pursuing this full potential?

Working with arousal—are you stressed, pressured, or motivated?

Most of us tend to think of stress as a uniformly bad thing in life, but the arousal theory suggests the key is finding your optimal level of stress rather than eliminating it entirely. How can we use the

Yerkes-Dodson Law to live more productive, healthy and happy lives?

You'll need to answer a few key questions first:

- What is your unique optimal level of arousal, generally speaking?

- How complex and familiar is the task you're trying to do?

- What are your skill levels and competencies relevant to the task at hand?

- Is stress and pressure in your life improving your performance or undermining it?

Stress, pressure and motivation can be understood as more or less the same quality, only at different intensities. Importantly, it's your *unique perception* of this intensity that matters. There are tests available to ascertain your level of stress and decide whether it's too high or low, but a formal test is not strictly necessary—you may be able to detect insufficient arousal levels by noticing disengagement or boredom, or diagnose excessive stress by the fact that you always feel completely burnt out.

Your goal is to find that sweet spot:

With an unchallenging and boring task and no time limit, your performance is likely to be average at best.

With a task that challenges you without overwhelming you, at a tight but doable deadline, you're "stressed" enough to put in the work and excel.

With a task that's unfamiliar, extremely difficult and way beyond our comfort zone and skill level, you'll do poorly or give up early on.

From this theory's point of view, the secret to finding optimal motivation for yourself doesn't lie in *you*, it lies in the nature of the *task*. If you want to inspire yourself, your job is to closely match your temperament and skill level with the difficulty of the task. Counterintuitively, it's people who stay comfortably in the middle zone who excel in the long term—those who are insufficiently aroused never amount to anything, while those who are too aroused risk burning out, quitting or seriously losing confidence.

Practice self-compassion, but temper it with the understanding that a little pressure now and then is good for you! If you're feeling undermotivated in life, consider whether it's because you are not really challenging yourself. Raise the stakes a little. Light that fire. Be honest if you've become sloppy in your work or taken things in your personal life for granted.

On the other hand, it's probably true that most of us in today's demanding world suffer from excessive rather than insufficient arousal. If on reflection you feel like life is grinding you down, there's a lot you can do—without necessarily quitting work or running away from responsibilities!

Firstly, find ways to increase your sense of *control* over what you do. Empower yourself by asking what you can change and focus on that—stress tends to melt once you pause and take a moment to consider all the options actually open to you. Secondly, try to bring more authenticity to life, whether it's in your hobbies, relationships or work. Speak your mind and express who you really are, and much of life's pressure seems to ease. Nothing is quite as draining as the effort needed to be who you aren't.

Break tasks into smaller chunks, slow down, and give yourself intermittent rewards. Quit the self-criticism habit. Remember that the difference between stress and pressure is simply one of degree—take your tasks and dial them back a bit. Make sure you feel competent with one activity before progressing to the next, more complex one.

Recognize when you are feeling overwhelmed, confused, or panicked and take a break to restructure the task in front of you. Mindfulness, positive affirmations, visualizations and simple deep breathing can help, too.

Finally, though it might seem ridiculous, use ritual and even superstition to boost your own confidence, focus and performance. A little prayer, a lucky coin or a special routine before a big decision or challenging task can actually have surprising effects. Sports psychology research done in 2010 by Cotterill and colleagues found that simple rituals like crossing the fingers actually had a notable effect on performance—go figure.

The Takeaway:

- There are three main theories of motivation: instinct theory, drives and needs theory, and personal arousal theory. We can use our newfound knowledge of all three to guide our actions.

- According to instinct theory, our actions and behaviors are governed by universal impulses deep within our psyche. We exhibit these behaviors without being taught to, and all animals express them in similar ways. There are different ideas of what exactly an instinct is, but generally they are considered biological urges that serve a particular purpose and help us survive and thrive in the world.

- The drives and needs theory is similar in that it claims our behaviors are motivated by certain needs, such as hunger. However, while we have instincts to do particular things, our needs give rise to certain drives that aim to fulfill our needs. Maslow's Hierarchy of Needs effectively summarizes the various needs a person has throughout his life and which ones are more important than others. While this stratification of importance varies between people, Maslow's pyramid is a good way to recognize our needs, and thus working toward fulfilling them.

- Arousal theory claims that we all have an optimal level of arousal, also called homeostasis. This arousal can stem from a variety of emotions such as happiness, stress, anger, satisfaction, etc. All of our behaviors are aimed at achieving or maintaining this optimal level. While too little arousal is obviously bad, too much can be harmful as well because both inhibit our performance and motivation levels.

- We can use all three theories together to maximize our own motivation: trust your gut feeling but temper it with more rational thought; consider your needs when dealing with yourself and others; make sure that you're hitting the Goldilocks zone where arousal is concerned— not too little, not too much. As you utilize all three frameworks, remember to constantly break down large tasks into smaller parts, get enough rest, and to take breaks when you feel overwhelmed.

Chapter 3: Hack Your Brain and Body

Your mind, emotions and body are instruments and the way you align and tune them determines how well you play life.

- *Harbhajan Singh Yogi*

Evolutionary Action

Evolutionary psychology is a popular framework for understanding present-day human behavior in terms of our ancient past. Evolutionarily speaking, behaviors and attributes develop only because they have historically improved our chances of survival as a species. Expanding on Charles Darwin's theories, thinkers and philosophers like Herbert Spencer began to imagine that social and psychological behaviors could also be understood in terms of their survival value, being retained by natural selection in the population at large.

Most of us would agree that millions of years of evolution has shaped humans into what they are. What does this mean for motivation? It means that we all possess "human nature"—the collection of physical, behavioral and emotional similarities we have in common with other humans because of our shared past. This is what it means to be a human, in all historical eras, all countries, all contexts.

By understanding our biological and evolutionary past, we understand what we're working with, and can devise a motivational strategy that respects where we came from.

Sounds great. But what about the things that make us unique?

Your life history and personal experiences interact with these inherited evolutionary characteristics. The external, environmental forces intermingle with the internal, personal ones. Your final behavior is determined both by your inherited predispositions or human nature, *and* by your own unique experiences, culture, family upbringing, personality, and so on. It's the "nature vs. nurture" idea—and it's not always easy to see what proportion has the most control over our behavior.

Today, most evolutionary theorists understand that traits—physiological or behavioral—are determined by a mix of factors. Motivation is no different. There is likely some portion of your current motivation status that is explained by innate, inherited factors, and some portion that is more malleable, coming down to your unique habits, history, personality, worldview, experience, and so on.

Evolutionary psychology is not without its criticisms. The "universal motives"—for example the human incentives around fear, sexual behavior, hygiene, control and social interaction—are arguably not so universal. Evolutionary psychology has been used to justify everything from economic greed and infidelity to racism and child abuse. Its basic assumption that all behaviors in some ways benefit natural or sexual selection mean that even the most horrifying impulses in humans can be considered advantageous in some way. The claim that modern observable human phenomena must have had some survival advantage in the past if they exist now is also simply false.

Nevertheless, how can an understanding of evolutionary psychology help us in our quest to develop our full potential? Without getting carried away by the finer theoretical nuances, one thing is clear: as humans, we are shaped both by nature and by nurture.

This means that we are not mere robots doomed to play out a fixed fate, but also that we are not completely at liberty to define ourselves as we will. For lasting personal development, we need to recognize our innate biological, physiological and evolutionary limitations—but that doesn't mean we don't have the scope to go far, far beyond these limits.

A simple example makes this clear. We now know that intelligence is at least *partly* inherited. In fact, it is not raw intelligence that is inherited, but a certain *capacity* or *potential*. This can be thought of as a rough range over which an individual can be expected to express themselves. Some people are born with wider ranges, some narrower; some people's ranges reach impressive feats, other people's don't.

However, the degree to which we fulfil this inherited potential comes down to our environment. If we grow and learn in an enriching and supportive environment, if we work hard, we find ourselves performing at the top limit of our inherited range, and vice versa. What this means is that a person with mediocre "nature" can outperform someone blessed in his area if they end up maxing out their "nurture."

We inherit a potential—but the extent to which we fulfil this potential has nothing to do with biology or evolution or culture or our families. It has to do with us and with the choices we make, right here and right now. In the rest of this chapter, we'll be using current knowledge about the limits and potentials of our biological selves to inform our efforts at becoming more motivated.

By understanding what motivation looks like on a *physiological level*, we give ourselves the best possible chance to perform optimally, and take control of ourselves on a *behavioral and emotional level.* Understanding our nature, we are better able to optimize our nurture. We'll look at the full complement of what humans have inherited from their evolutionary past, such as our neuroscience and biological rhythms. Because once we understand the "matter," we can more intelligently move on to "mind over matter."

So far, we've spoken about motivation causing "behavior" without looking too closely at what that behavior is. Motivation is *expressed*—not just through decision-making but through our language, gestures, and facial expressions. Motivation can vary in intensity and quality, and play out cognitively in our thoughts and attention, and in our emotional engagement with what's in front of us.

We tend to think that motivation is purely an abstract, psychological state of affairs, but in fact *motivation is embodied, with several psychophysiological expressions.*

When you're motivated, you're also physiologically aroused, with a resulting hormonal profile, for example increased levels of cortisol. Your heart and blood vessels may respond to a challenging task as much as your mind does. Your pupil size, blink-rate and eye movements may show subtle changes to keep up, and tiny electrical changes flash across the surface of your skin. Your entire musculature, skeletal structure, and facial expression can shift with changing stimulation and stress levels.

We shouldn't be surprised by the fact that motivation is not just a brain state—the brain is, after all, just one part of your body. Your neural activity will flow depending on your motivational state, recruiting every part of your brain. With a fuller view that acknowledges the body, **motivation can be** seen as an **ebbing and flowing state of arousal that expresses itself through thoughts, emotions, and behavior**. All of this expression is directed toward one end: achieving the goals that come with satisfying our needs.

Researcher Sung-il Kim proposed a model in 2013 to bring these disparate processes together. Kim's process consisted of three subprocesses: first **building** motivation, then **sustaining** motivation, and finally the process of **regulating** motivation.

Generating motivation is driven by the expectation of reward, and activates the ventral striatum in the brain—a largely automatic and unconscious process.

The next step, however, is to sustain motivation, and this comes down to making decisions based on value judgments, and evaluating the effect of certain behaviors against your goals. During this process, the striatum and orbitofrontal cortex are recruited. Behaviors that reinforce the value of what you're doing are invaluable in sustaining motivation. Receiving encouragement from external sources such as friends and support groups, and even grading yourself on your progress, are both good ways to keep motivation going.

For the final step, motivation is regulated consciously via cognitive and goal-directed control. For these, we need high-level cognitive skills—planning, adapting, monitoring, etc.—which are associated with the anterior cingulate cortex of the brain. Using these skills to track your progress and engage in future strategy selection are good ways to regulate your motivation.

You may decide to join a training course initially because of the (probably unconscious) associations of the course with better work performance. You maintain your interest and motivation during the course by appealing to more formally stated values: you work hard, you care about professional development, you don't like quitting (and also it would be a bit embarrassing...). Finally, you regulate this behavior by regularly finding ways to use what you learn at your job, to check in with your progress on the course, and so on.

These three steps work seamlessly together, suggesting a way that behavioral aspects of motivation can be mapped onto neurophysiological aspects.

Like the model we considered in an earlier chapter, motivation stitches together antecedent conditions from our environment that stimulate us to generate a motivation toward something, and then these motives (emotional, cognitive or needs-based) help strengthen this motivation and maintain it, so that the desired goal is met when we take appropriate actions toward it—i.e. there are changes in your behavior, physiology, or levels of engagement inspired by your new motivation.

Most motivation models contain these three rough elements: a. **initiate**—the instigating stimulus or generation of motivation, b. **persist**—the building and sustaining of this motive, and c. **organize**—the regulation that comes with seeing actions play out in the world toward certain goals.

By understanding these three separate components of the motivation process, we can diagnose motivation problems, by asking if any of these areas are lacking somehow. If we only focus on one of these aspects or processes, we may be missing important issues elsewhere, or overlook opportunities to improve.

Whether we frame motivation in terms of a "flow" state, an expression or management of drives, a question of ego development or arousal, a psychological phenomenon or purely biological and based on survival, or consider it in terms of needs, one thing is certain: motivation is multifaceted. If we hope to grasp the concept and optimize our own motivation, we need techniques that acknowledge its complexity.

Motivation is not just about the cognitive aspects of the brain. It's about the rise and fall of arousal across the entire organism. Consider the following example: A man takes up bodybuilding. The answer to why he does this is complex.

Biologically and evolutionarily speaking, as a man he has more muscle mass than a woman, more testosterone and a complement of evolved behaviors that emphasize strength and physical prowess.

Emotionally, he was bullied as a teen and now derives satisfaction of his self-esteem needs by proving to others that he is capable and even intimidating.

Neurologically, he gets a massive dopamine and serotonin rush every time he trains, and a wide range of brain regions and neurotransmitter pathways are activated as he cements this habit, forming positive associations in his reward centers.

Socially and culturally, he forms friendships with other bodybuilders that fulfil his needs for affiliation and belonging, and often gets compliments on his physique.

You get the idea. There is no single motivation for this man's decision to initiate, sustain and organize his bodybuilding behavior—rather, motivation takes on many different forms and guises. The environment can instigate interest or generate a motivation that can be sustained on multiple levels, mediated by biochemical and neurological agents, and finally revealing itself in the form of concrete behavior.

How do we use this information to our advantage?

We acknowledge and work *with* our biology.

It's never a matter of sheer willpower or a few magic hacks, but more a question of taking conscious control of the physiological processes that underlie our motivation, so we can achieve the goals we want to. Just like the man who took up bodybuilding, we have many factors motivating us. We just need to know what they are before using them to our advantage. Practically, you can take a few steps to make sure you're not setting yourself up to fail before you've even started.

It's old advice, but get enough good quality sleep. Properly resting your brain is non-negotiable for optimal motivation, and no amount of external incentivizing will overcome a body and mind that's simply exhausted. In a similar way, avoid extreme caloric deficits or excesses—i.e. eat moderately. Maintain stable sugar levels with plenty of whole grains and fiber to slow digestion—the idea is to prevent your attention dipping into survival concerns when you need it to focus on something better!

Make sure you're getting enough vitamin D, do aerobic exercise regularly and re-evaluate your general environment—are there any relationships, behaviors or untreated conditions (including things like depression) that are sapping your motivation?

The Almighty Dopamine

To survive, humans are motivated to act toward what they need, and away from pain and danger. Simple, right? But how does the human body decide which is which? It uses a neurochemical system called a reward system—of which the primary communicator is the neurotransmitter dopamine.

Every time you process a stimulus as a reward, you do so because dopamine produced in your ventral tegmental area communicates with your nucleus accumbens. And when you experience a reward, you are motivated to repeat the behavior that caused it. Neurons light up in *expectation* that the same thing will happen again, and we lay down memories that cement those associations.

The mesolimbic dopamine pathway essentially works with feedback loops—you are able to predict rewards because your brain learns to recognize that something important is going to happen soon, activating dopamine release. This happens *before* we receive our reward—meaning that dopamine encourages and motivates us using the anticipation of a reward that we've learnt about.

Dopamine used to be associated with pleasure, but now the Castellón group and John Salamone at the University of Connecticut are changing this paradigm, investigating why dopamine is also released in stressful situations. The conclusion many neuroscientists have come to is that **dopamine is all about motivation and appraising risk and potential reward,** rather than pleasure.

Dopamine helps us remember, process emotions, learn, plan and reason. And it helps the brain orchestrate all of that toward goal-directed behavior; dopamine is the neurochemical expression of motivation. "Reward learning" teaches us to anticipate rewards when we undertake certain behaviors.

Interestingly, there are individual variations in reward systems—some people are extra sensitive to rewards, while others respond more to punishments. A study done at Vanderbilt University found that extroverted high achievers often have greater dopamine signalling in the brain regions associated with motivation and reward. Furthermore, there are variations in how people balance perceived reward against perceived risk when deciding to act.

Developmental life stage matters—as people grow older, the brain regions responsible for emotional self-regulation also mature. If someone has a dysregulation in their reward system, they may demonstrate addiction and aggression, or else inappropriate docility—i.e., a faulty arousal response to stimuli in the environment. In fact, dopamine insufficiency has been associated with lack of motivation in conditions like fibromyalgia, Parkinson's and multiple sclerosis.

Circadian Rhythms

The biology of motivation is not simply a *what* but also a *when*.

The difference between high and low motivation may simply be a matter of time. Circadian rhythms are the body's "inner clock" or cycles of when to wake, sleep and eat. Prompted by cues like sunlight or temperature, our circadian rhythm can powerfully affect how energized we feel. These rhythms are coordinated in the suprachiasmatic nucleus in the hypothalamus. For example, when cells in the eyes detect a drop in light, signals travel to the suprachiasmatic nucleus, which encourages the production of melatonin, thus instigating sleep.

Your body can only do one thing at a time, and the circadian rhythm is a way of allotting different essential survival needs (sleeping, eating, and even sex) to different times of day. Being drowsy when you planned to study might not feel like "motivation," but it is—it's your body's biochemical motivation to undertake essential rest at the optimal time.

Pushing against your body's natural rhythms has been associated with sleep disorders, depression, obesity and, most interestingly, attention and concentration difficulties. It's not rocket science: forcing yourself to do a lot of hard, complex work when your body is doing everything it can to sleep is a recipe for disaster. You'll know that your sleep cycles are out of whack if you frequently experience insomnia or daytime sleepiness, not to mention brain fog and lack of energy. As you might expect by now, there are individual differences in circadian rhythm, too.

Your "chronotype" is your unique sleep personality, i.e. whether you're more of a morning person or night owl, or something in between. There are four chronotypes: the bear, the lion, the wolf, and the dolphin. Bears are people whose circadian rhythms mimic the movement of the sun. They're up the earliest, and feel a dip in energy levels by afternoon. Lions are early risers too, though not as early as bears. Wolves prefer late starts to the day and belong to the nocturnal end of the spectrum. Finally, dolphins do not have any fixed sleeping pattern.

To find out which one you are, all you need to do is carefully document your energy levels and sleep habits for a week or two to identify the times of day you feel most and least energized. Then, as much as is possible, assign novel or high-energy tasks to your most motivated periods while resting or doing mundane tasks at other times. Alternatively, you could try discovering your chronotype through trial and error. Make minor changes to the structure of your days and observe which ones leave you feeling most productive and energetic. Keep experimenting till you hit the sweet spot.

Whatever your optimal schedule, it's important to keep it consistent, and wake and sleep at roughly the same time each day. Your biology takes its cues from the environment—so avoid an environment brimming with harsh, unnatural light from devices late at night. After all, our ancestors' bodies evolved to live in worlds naturally lit by the rise and fall of the sun. When you wake up, try to expose yourself to natural light and plenty of fresh air—a morning walk is ideal.

The main question running along throughout this book is, "How do I motivate myself" or perhaps, "How do I motivate others?"

Hopefully, in some of the discussion above, you're starting to see that the answer to this question is: "Create an environment that naturally supports the cognitive, emotional and physical aspects of healthy motivation."

Your motivational state cannot be separated out from your environment—

whether that's your social, emotional or cultural context, or all of them. Your brain is completely intertwined with the world it lives in, and so, if we want to enhance its function, we can't help but to consider the surrounding environment that affects that function.

Much of the early personal development-style writing done on motivation focused only on the cognitive aspects—willpower and tough love and smart goals. But this is a very limited view of a rather complex process.

Many parts of our motivational processes may indeed be hidden from our conscious awareness, so that we're not even completely sure of why we behave as we do. Blithely forging ahead with a commitment to be more disciplined is likely to fail until we consider the emotional, possible unconscious antecedents of our actual behavior.

Some ways of thinking about motivation encourage us to imagine that we are isolated entities, acting completely freely against a neutral, unconnected backdrop.

But in reality, it's more the case that we are constantly engaged in a dynamic *conversation with our environment*, mutually affecting one another.

Your environment certainly affects you (for example, you may live in a country with low winter light that influences your melatonin levels, depression and motivation), but you can also impact your environment (you can move or buy a therapy light). As a person, you look to the environment to fill your needs, and act accordingly. But your environment in turn has its own demands, limits, opportunities, and so on. These shape your needs and correspondingly, your behavior.

Every time you engage with your world, formulate a goal, take action, appraise your results and adjust before feeding back and trying again, you are in communication with your environment. If you consistently take actions that foster an environment that best supports your motivation and goal-attainment, you will set up a positive feedback loop, reinforcing beneficial behaviors over time.

The principle is simple but not easy: to change ourselves, we change the environment we inhabit.

In a way, this turns a lot of attitudes about motivation upside down. It's not about white-knuckling your way to better productivity, or valorizing hard work and talent. As important as these are, it may be that environment matters more than raw talent or effort.

Seemingly small environmental features (like number of daylight hours) can actually have enormous and far-reaching effects. For example, Greenland has the highest suicide rate in the world, and never-ending daylight hours during summer as well as clashes between traditional Inuit and Western culture are some of the commonly cited reasons.

Talent, hard work and enthusiasm certainly play a role in motivation. But personal attributes and behaviors may only be a portion of the story (nature), while the nurture portion may ultimately have more influence. So, if this is the case, what does the optimal environment for staying motivated look like? And to what extent can we influence this environment ourselves?

One simple way technique is to automate as many decisions as possible. Make the environment make good decisions for you, consistently. For example, install productivity apps to limit social media use, have a habit of never keeping unhealthy snacks in the home, get your vitamins delivered on a monthly subscription and connect with an accountability team that will show up at your doorstep when it's time to train, no excuses.

Piggyback new habits on old ones so you're expending less mental energy and effort to stick with them. Park a good distance from your office so you're naturally fitting in an extra thirty-minute walk every day without even trying, for example. Make sure that you don't have to go out of your way to incorporate new habits. Pick a gym that's on the way home from work, or if you want to learn a new instrument, keep it in a place that's easily visible so you're constantly reminded of it. Honestly appraise your environment—if you're failing to summon up motivation, is it actually a sign of a poor, unsupportive environment? Put your energies into improving what's lacking.

These improvements can be made on all levels, from the mundane to the profound, and in all areas of life, from relationships to work to personal development. Examples:

- Crafting a comfortable, appealing workspace—think healthy snacks, nice décor, a comfy chair, an uncluttered workplace, noise-cancelling earphones...
- Finding creative ways to mitigate stress from your cultural environment, for example installing apps to prevent yourself from "doom scrolling" and subscribing to high-quality news sites and blogs rather than wasting time on social media.
- Developing a strong social environment, e.g. a weekly session with a counselor, regular time out with close friends, date nights with a partner, and a call once in a while to your mom—all to help you feel

grounded, supported and witnessed as you embark on life's challenges.

- Moving to a different place or switching jobs to something that suits your innate talents and preferences better.
- Changing your diet, exercise routine or sleep schedule.
- Seeking intellectual and creative stimulus in the form of challenging new reading material, inspiring art and documentaries, or a religious or spiritual retreat where you feel encouraged to pursue higher goals.
- Committing to a yearly checkup so you can catch and treat any vitamin deficiencies.

Rubber Hits the Road

Let's put it all together. Remember, theory means nothing until it's put into *action*. Here's how:

Dopamine

It's not about willpower—it's about dopamine! You'll know you're running low when you feel apathetic and low on energy and enthusiasm. Fatigue, forgetfulness, apathy, distractibility, insomnia, lack of concentration and even sugar cravings are signs you could use a boost.

How can we use what we know about the "motivation chemical" to support our own motivation?

Firstly, you need to *create rewarding experiences to supply your reward system feedback loops.* Rather than this dampening your enthusiasm, you're actually more likely to work hard.

- Set small goals and take a moment to celebrate when you achieve them, fostering feelings of accomplishment.
- Visualize the realization of your final goal, revelling in the positive emotions.
- Brag. Well, maybe not brag—but share your achievements and get support and praise.

- Use productivity and organizational tools to help your process stay lean and focused.
- Don't multitask!
- Take frequent breaks—a short nap, or a quick workout to get your blood flowing will boost dopamine levels, even if they're not associated with the main task.
- Set process goals where possible, so your effort is always rewarded, even if you don't quite achieve your goal.
- If your motivation is flagging, simply commit to doing five minutes at first. The satisfaction of having completed just those five minutes can be enough to propel you to do more.

But you can also boost dopamine levels in other ways, and start reinforcing feedback loops that trigger, sustain and shape your motivation for any goal. One easy thing to do is eat more protein. The amino acid tyrosine is necessary for the production of dopamine in your brain, but can also be synthesized from another amino acid, phenylalanine. Very low levels of these amino acids can cause dopamine drops, but you can fix this by taking in high-protein foods, or tyrosine-rich foods like avocados, almonds and bananas.

Saturated fat intake has been tentatively associated with lower dopamine levels—i.e. foods like animal fat, butter and palm oil—independent of other parameters like body weight or hormone levels. This may be because of the inflammation these foods cause, which in turn damages the brain's reward system.

The gut (i.e. the "second brain") produces neurotransmitters too, including dopamine. There is some limited evidence suggesting that certain strains of gut microbacteria can positively impact mood and motivation., so a probiotic supplement or fermented foods in the diet may help. In fact, the consumption of velvet beans may raise dopamine levels since they contain a chemical precursor to dopamine.

Other beneficial lifestyle interventions are what you might expect: exercise regularly to boost dopamine, increase blood flow and fill your body with oxygen. Returning to the question of sleep, good quality rest is important, since dopamine is released in high levels first thing in the morning to encourage alertness—except if you've had poor sleep the night before. Aim for seven to nine hours with good sleep hygiene.

Whatever you do, try to avoid unhealthy ways to temporarily spike dopamine—such as with caffeine, nicotine or sugary processed foods. This could only spur addiction that saps motivation in the long run. Some supplements such as ashwagandha and panax ginseng can help with focus and energy and are natural and healthy.

Finally, make sure your life is filled with enough time for rest, contemplation and enjoyment. Meditate, get a stress-busting massage, make liberal use of calming or inspiring music, and expose yourself to natural sunlight, fresh air, and as much nature as you can.

It may seem like these vague lifestyle improvements couldn't possibly make a significant enough difference to your overall goals or motivation levels, but it all adds up. Every conscious choice toward constructing a supportive environment will help your own innate motivation to come shining to the fore.

Circadian rhythms

It's not just about sleep. Your internal twenty-four-hour clock tells you when to do *everything*, including when to be motivated and attentive. Your internal ebbs and flows are delicate and respond to the environment—which is precisely why you need to be careful that the modern world isn't throwing your natural flow out of whack.

Under-sleeping, staring at screens for hours, eating processed junk, stressing, being sedentary, alcohol, nicotine and caffeine—it all adds up. To bring yourself back into a natural circadian rhythm, you need to create an environment that supports the inner schedule your body evolved to follow.

That means plenty of natural light exposure (i.e., not staring at a smartphone screen at three a.m. in the dark), plenty of fresh air (breathe deeply outside in nature) and plenty of good-quality sleep at the right times. Keep your room free of things that beep and glow in the night, and make sure that you're winding down gently before bed with yoga, reading or meditation. Avoid excess caffeine, especially in the afternoons, and most importantly, stick to a daily sleep routine and wake and sleep at the same time each day.

Your circadian rhythm is regular and consistent—match its pace by not just sleeping but eating at the same times each day, with heavier meals earlier on. Exercise regularly and at roughly the same time each day, according to your peak energy levels. Have a daily stress management routine to help you calm down at the end of the day. None of this is supremely complicated, but it might take some effort at first, since the modern always-on world seems to constantly push us to be wired and productive 24/7.

If you're a go-getting Type A, you might unconsciously worry that too much downtime will compromise your productivity. Relax—the reverse is true.

Moving *with* your circadian rhythms actually makes you more resilient, productive, happy and healthy. You have permission to chill out.

Creating an environment for success

One of the easiest ways to hack your motivation via your body is to exercise. We all already know that regular exercise is non-negotiable. There's very little that it doesn't improve! Exercise has consistently been proven to lift mood, boost self-esteem, cut your disease risk and all-around improve energy levels.

The release of endorphins doesn't just make you feel good; the extra feeling of being alert and energized after a workout is pure motivation energy for the rest of life. Exercise boosts neurogenesis in the brain and increases the size of the hippocampus, which is the area associated with learning and memory.

It doesn't matter what your other goals or aspirations are, if you are exercising regularly, you are maintaining your body in a peak state of alert, resilient wellness that will translate to better focus and discipline. And you don't have to go all out—researchers at the University of Copenhagen have found it's *moderate* exercise that has the best overall health effects, so you're far better off balancing workouts with plenty of daily stress management and quality rest.

With all these different potential lifestyle improvements, where do you even start? It doesn't have to be overwhelming. Begin with noting down just a few areas that are weighing most on your mind at the moment—no more than three. Next, visualize what it might actually look like for you to achieve some desired outcome in these areas.

Flesh it out in your mind's eye. Next, brainstorm some practical ways that you can close the distance between that end point and where you are now. Finally, focus only on the very next step that you can take to get on the path toward that goal. Not the next five steps—just the next practical single thing you can do, right now. Then, hone in on that.

It can be overwhelming to try and incorporate a whole range of lifestyle changes all at once, but it's easier if you zoom in on just those that have the greatest chance of impacting your life. You don't need to solve it all in one day. You just need to take positive action right here, today. Tomorrow, you can do it again. But for today, just focus on the action that will bring you closer to your envisioned goal.

The Takeaway:

- Evolutionary theory has taught us that most of our behaviors have come about because they ensure that we survive with changing times. Yet these natural endowments from nature are complimented by individual traits that make us unique. We can use this dichotomy to motivate ourselves by realizing where our strengths and weaknesses lie and developing them accordingly.
- Motivation can be seen as an ebbing and flowing state of arousal that expresses itself through thoughts,

emotions, and behavior. To incorporate these disparate elements of motivation, Sung Il-Kim has suggested a tripartite framework that can help us utilize each of these components of motivation. According to this framework, there are three parts to cultivating motivation: generating it, sustaining it, and regulating it. By following this trajectory, we fire up the relevant parts of our brain that motivate us, which has a corresponding physiological effect that arouses us into action.

- Three factors play a large role in helping you generate, sustain, and regulate motivation. These are your dopamine levels, circadian rhythm, and exercise.

- Dopamine is a neurotransmitter that plays a central role in the reward system of your brain. When you receive a reward for doing something, your brain releases dopamine and sets up a feedback loop which expects similar rewards in the future. By supplying yourself with rewards for completing goals and tasks, you can hack your internal reward system to motivate yourself.

- Your circadian rhythm is your internal body clock which determines the hours of the day where you're most active and attentive, when you feel sluggish, and when is the right time for you to rest. Some of us like to rise early, while others prefer sleeping in. Shape your routine according to your preferences for maximum productivity.

- Lastly, exercise is also an invaluable way to improve your concentration and increase serotonin. This has a tremendous impact on motivation levels, so make sure you exercise at least moderately several times each week.

Chapter 4: The Mindset for Motivation

Ability is what you're capable of doing. Motivation determines what you do. Attitude determines how well you do it.

- *Lou Holtz*

Now that we've laid the biological, evolutionary and neurochemical foundation for our motivation and behavior (and hopefully made some positive changes), we can consider the realm of motivation that most people typically begin with: the *mind* of the motivated person.

What are the psychological and personality differences between a motivated and unmotivated person?

All else being equal, what will distinguish a motivate person from someone who simply doesn't give a damn?

A personality trait is a fixed pattern of behavior, regardless of changing situation or environment. Psychologists have formed several theories to capture the personality range of human beings, but an early and still popular model is the "Big Five" or OCEAN model, to describe a person's degree of Openness, Conscientiousness, Extraversion, Agreeableness and Neuroticism.

It's not hard to imagine how these different traits might impact a person's motivation in life:

Being **open to experience**, we allow ourselves to envision new possible goals with curiosity and interest.

Being **conscientious**, we commit to a deliberate and ordered approach to achieving these goals.

Being **extraverted**, we seek arousal and actively pursue the things we want.

Being **agreeable**, we work well with others and cooperate toward shared goals.

Being **neurotic**, we work hard to avoid punishment and negative experience.

A motivated person, then, is someone who is open-minded and adventurous, hard-working and diligent, extraverted, sufficiently sociable and yes, a little "neurotic" (or at least knows how to channel anxiety!).

Remedying a lack of motivation could be a question of trying to cultivate these traits in yourself. Are there any attitudes, mindsets, beliefs or personality quirks that are working against you? We're all guilty of these at least some of the time:

- Pessimism and seeing the worst in everything—for example never starting something because you doubt your ability to succeed. The remedy is to be proactive, to take risks and to take a hard, honest look at the situation, and what you can do to improve it if it's genuinely a problem.

- Forgetting optimism—not quite the same as being pessimistic! It's hard to be motivated when goal-achieving seems so joyless. Boost your dopamine with mini-rewards and remind yourself of all the exciting reasons why you wanted to improve in the first place.

- Being too grandiose—like planning to lose forty pounds in a month. It's easier to motivate yourself to do something small ten times than to do one massive thing once. Break it down. Start small.

- Expecting rewards before hard work—once you've set your goal, return your focus to the here and now, where the hard work happens. Don't expect miracles!

- Shirking responsibility—nobody else can take action on your behalf. Drop blame and take responsibility. When you take charge of your own time and resources, proactively make choices and stand by the consequences, you are empowered to do your best. No matter what.

- Low self-esteem—some people feel deep down that they're just not worth striving for more, or that they're not fit to the challenge of achieving their dreams. Small goals can help here, too. Mini-goals will give you plenty of proof that you *can* do something.

Things like excessive social media use, addictive substances, distracting games, TV, bad lifestyle habits, etc. are not in themselves personality traits, but if you find your life filled with them and they're sapping your motivation, you may want to question what's keeping them there. Certain personality traits may predispose us to weaknesses when it comes to motivation—but with clarity and awareness we can work to strengthen these aspects of our personalities.

If you've covered all your *physiological* bases and still experience motivation blocks, try asking yourself the following questions to narrow in on what's holding you back:

1. *What do you really want?*

Let's cut to the chase. If you can't answer immediately and with conviction, you've found your problem. You may be lacking clarity. How can you work toward something if you're not even sure what it is? Fuzzy next steps can make you stall and procrastinate. Go back to the drawing board and try to uncover an answer to this question that energizes and excites you. Think about what kind of goals fit in with your values and what you know you need to improve about yourself. We all realize our own deepest shortcomings. Recognize them, and then let that inspire sharp, focused goals.

2. *What stories are you telling yourself about yourself?*

It's useless acting toward a goal when internally you're cutting yourself down, self-criticizing and writing off your efforts before you've even begun. Your inner critic can drain the life out of you. Ask honestly if you've made underachieving, risk-averse behavior a part of your identity. It might be time to start changing the script. On a related note, many of us are uninspired simply because we've underestimated ourselves and set goals that are too small. Trust yourself to thrive under a bit of challenge!

3. *Are you trying to make quantum leaps?*

You want your goal, and you want it now. Awesome! But this can make you intolerant for the daily, sometimes mundane job of piecing your goal together, bit by bit. Whether you're overwhelmed and burnt out, or just totally put off by how large the task is, you need to scale it down to manageable chunks and tackle just one at a time. Commit to the smallest action you can make a consistent habit.

4. *Are you trying to avoid hard work?*

Sometimes, there is no magic formula or deep-seated childhood psychological excuse to explain your procrastination. Sometimes, it's just 100 percent pure laziness! It's easy to commit to a goal when you only visualize the end point. But you need to establish solid daily routines that are ingrained in habit. You need to work at your goal consistently, and this takes discipline. If this is challenging, you may need to find ways to give yourself intermittent rewards, so you stay the course rather than lose interest along the way. Alternatively, if you find achieving a goal exhausting, now may not be the right time for it. Switch to a goal you're more motivated to pursue and reserve this one for later.

5. *Are you unmotivated or are you afraid?*

Goals, especially big ones, can seem overwhelming and intimidating to even the best of us. In such cases it's easy to look at all the progress you need to make and feel like giving up before you've even started. Fear can keep you pulling back from unknown situations, including new opportunities and your dreams and goals. It's not unusual to feel fear, but try not to let it drive your decisions. Look at it closely. Get into dialogue with your fear and try to dismantle it—is it a legitimate concern or is it merely based on negative self-talk and poor self-esteem?

Similarly, you can't force yourself to be motivated. Desire for a certain outcome, no matter how strong, doesn't necessarily motivate you to achieve it. That comes with discipline and doing instead of merely thinking. You'll find that once you make yourself do things, you'll enjoy them more than you anticipated. This will motivate you to continue completing those tasks in the future.

6. *Are you striving toward someone else's goal?*

We are all influenced externally, but your goals should also be ones that are meaningful to you personally. It's hard to find motivation if your stated goals are actually inauthentic, or clash with other equally important values you hold. Remember that incentives are not the same as motivation. Are you moving toward something or merely away from something?

The Extrinsic and Intrinsic

The last question on that list can be particularly illuminating. In a world where plenty of people are eager to tell you what you should want and why, it can be hard to tune into your own, genuinely meaningful desires.

Intrinsic motivation comes from within, and is inspired by the satisfaction of our own needs, and our desire for growth. When you are internally motivated, you work harder and with more persistence and creativity. You dig into challenges of all kinds more thoroughly, giving yourself a richer understanding than if you'd simply been compelled to pay attention by an external motivator.

Intrinsic motivation has rightly been associated with greater work and interpersonal success, more resilient psychological health, greater self-esteem and self-image, higher energy levels and feelings of empowerment, and fewer bad habits like addictions. Most importantly, being motivated from within simply has a greater chance of allowing you to actually achieve what you set out to.

Extrinsic motivation is driven by rewards such as money, fame, good grades, praise, etc. You do things to gain something other than your own personal satisfaction. While extrinsic motivation can give rise to intrinsic motivation or be useful by itself, this is often short-lived. So, if you're being promised a lot of money for a task you don't want to do, you might manage to push yourself to do it because earning money extrinsically motivates you. However, nobody can sustain themselves long-term on extrinsic motivation. Eventually, you'll need your own needs and desires to derive fulfilment from whatever it is you're doing.

You are intrinsically motivated when you:

- Read a book because you're curious about what it could teach you
- Tidy the house because like love feeling clean and organized
- Spend time with your family because you love them

You are extrinsically motivated when you:

- Read a book because it will be tested in the exam
- Tidy the house because your partner gets mad if you don't
- Spend time with your family because you need to ask them for a favor afterwards

The only difference between internal and external motivation is *the source that energizes the behavior*, but the truth is that no external incentive could make you pursue a goal with as much energy as genuinely wanting it from within.

We've covered internal and external motivation in a previous section in the book, but realistically the two can and do overlap. You may have a genuine inner need for connectedness to other people, for example, but it can be tricky to untangle that from praise and admiration that comes from the outside.

You may be wondering: if the behavior ultimately gets done, does it *really* matter what the source of motivation is?

It turns out, it does. Your attitude to your tasks and your perception of the source of motivation make a huge difference. The now recognized "overjustification effect" proves this—children who are externally rewarded for doing an activity they already expressed an innate desire to do, actually lose interest in that activity. It's as though adding an external incentive cheapens the experience. After all, aren't we only externally motivated when something is so undesirable, we wouldn't do it without a reward?

Though intrinsic motivation is preferable, there's a time and a place for extrinsic motivation—if you're only willing to unclog the toilet when you're inspired by a genuine inner motivation, you'll be waiting for a long time! Extrinsic motivation works great for minor tasks that can be completed without much effort. However, long-term tasks and goals need intrinsic motivation for success.

External motivation often comes in the form of valuable feedback, or as a way to inspire excitement for things despite a lack of discipline or natural interest. You may need a little external motivation simply to get through a dull part of a task, or to discipline yourself to stay on track with the previous goal instead of running off after the next interesting one.

Both types of motivation are useful. It's OK to try external motivation when you're naturally lacking in enthusiasm for something you know is good for you, or to get through rough patches. *Don't* use it for something you're already motivated to do (i.e. turn play into work). Be careful—extrinsic rewards may get the job done, but intrinsic motivation will drop as a result. This is somewhat less the case when external rewards are unexpected and come after the behavior.

Finally, some external rewards do increase internal motivation—for example, praise. Positive feedback and compliments can build self-esteem and a sense of competence, which makes autonomous and goal-driven behavior more likely next time. It's a fine line, though—praise (and any external reward) should be felt to be an *acknowledgment* of hard work, and not the sole *reason* the behavior was done in the first place.

A reward can work because it creates positive emotional associations in our brains. The pleasure associated with the reward stimulates dopamine release, which reinforces the behavior and may create positive feedback loops that cement the conditioned behavior. But again, this needs to be weighed up with the "hidden cost." You may force the desired behavior, but intrinsic motivation drops, so that when the reward/punishment is removed, the drive to do the behavior is even lower than before.

Look at your own behavior and examine what's energizing it. A healthy relationship to external rewards and punishments is to see them as a tool to bridge the gaps in your intrinsic motivation. Extrinsic motivations, when used correctly, can help shape and support intrinsic motivation, rather than weaken and undermine it.

It's all in the attitude. Behaviors in themselves are not intrinsically or extrinsically motivated. It all comes down to *your perception* of the reason for doing something.

When you were a child, you had an innate motivation that soon became tied up with external forces and pressures. Intrinsic motivation came first, but you developed extrinsic motivation with the help of your parents and teachers.

Healthy adults have found a productive and comfortable balance between the two. Problems can arise when a person relies too heavily on external approval (and has zero personal motivation), or when they don't respond to external motivation at all (can you imagine the behavior of someone who literally doesn't care what anyone thinks, including their employers, friends... or the police?), or when they lack both (a completely apathetic person with no drive at all).

If you had overprotective and fearful parents, you might have learnt the lesson that exploration and curiosity were dangerous, dampening your innate motivation and replacing it with external motivators (i.e. theirs). You may become the typical "people pleaser" who is unable to take risks. If you had plenty of non-specific praise ("you're my perfect little angel"), you actually had very little to motivate you. Why make an effort when you're already perfect? It's *specific* praise that reinforces the idea that outcomes are under your control ("you did so well because you worked so hard!").

Too much external reward can weaken your own motivation, whether it's a pattern learnt from childhood or your current life. Ask yourself: do you feel empowered to pursue your own independent goals? Can you feel good about yourself no matter how other people value or don't value you? If not, you may need to work to strengthen your inner motivation:

- Identify your efforts and give yourself credit for them
- Give yourself *specific* positive feedback
- Reward yourself for making progress at regular intervals

- Find ways to regulate your mood or lack of motivation, such as meditation
- Tap into what truly energizes and empowers you, and drop what doesn't
- Tell your friends about your goals to combine intrinsic and extrinsic motivation

Finding a better balance between the two kinds of motivation starts with honest awareness of how you're currently motivated in life. Intrinsic is always better, but extrinsic has its uses, especially when certain factors are outside of your control.

Go for intrinsic motivation for the large, long-term, overarching aspects of your life (i.e. the career or life partner you choose), but extrinsic motivation is fine for getting through life's brief but unavoidable details (unclogging that stupid toilet).

When you can't muster up motivation, look to the smart use of external rewards, incentives or (as a last resort) punishments. If you can, combine extrinsic and intrinsic. Pick a meaningful goal based on your own needs, and use occasional external motivation to get you through sluggish periods along the way.

If you have two equal competing intrinsic goals, pick the one that comes with the most external rewards—but the *external reward is best viewed as a boost or bonus, and not a core feature* of any decision.

We've seen that our behavior is in constant conversation with our environment. How you balance internal and external will depend on this environment, on your personality, the task at hand, your skillset and familiarity, your gut instinct, and much more. But the great thing is, the more you understand about yourself, the more you take an active part in the process, and direct it toward the results you want.

The Stages of Change Model

Motivation is needed to inspire action. But what action?

In the grand scheme, action means **change**, and the implied change is one for the better.

If you're reading this book, you're almost certainly wanting to find ways not just to act, but to *be better*. The link between motivation and success is key—and it may be stronger than the impact of raw talent or intelligence.

The trouble with change is that you're already an expert at being the way you are. It takes effort and hard work to break out of old habits and learn new, better ones.

This effort is motivation, and we've seen that it can come from many sources. We need initial inspiration, the drive to persist despite difficulty, real focus, adaptability, resilience and grit. All of us want to be better. But not all of us have what it takes to propel us into the new potential we desire.

Motivation is not just the initial spark, it's the quality that allows you to undertake all the steps required to make a positive, lasting change. Motivations can be internal or external, positive or negative. An internal positive motivator could be passion and self-actualization, but a negative external one could be pressure and punishment from others, and so on. While any of the four combinations can lead to change, it's **internal positive motivators** that have the highest chance of creating change *and* happiness.

Once you've identified your motivation source, examine your effort level: does your effort match the stated goal? If not, you may need to lower your goal or up your effort—but something's gotta give. Many of us have bought into the myth that success is easy and attainable if you're a talented genius, or if you're seeking a goal you *really* want. But the truth is, at some point, you just need to work.

Here, your ability to push through the slog is what distinguishes you from the people who give up. No, you don't have to love it. You don't have to be "inspired." All you have to do is keep working! Your attitude is key: struggle isn't a sign that anything is wrong. Difficulty is merely part of the process—there's no getting around it, only *through* it.

To get you through you need clear, well-defined goals, and a deliberate commitment to achieving them. Giving your all and working with dedication no matter what—this is the *result* of having laid the groundwork, asked yourself the hard questions and unpicked your real desires, needs, limiting beliefs, and unique strengths.

Some people make the mistake of seeing an ultra-motivated person and thinking it's enough to merely mimic their dedication; but their dedication came as a result of their self-knowledge, courage, self-compassion, intelligent planning and insight. *That's* what makes it so effective.

Draw power and resilience from understanding and owning your **strengths**: write down a list of your personal attributes that will serve you well. Celebrate and embrace them.

Stay humbled and balanced by remembering your **weaknesses and limitations**: add these to the list and accept them too, knowing that real change comes from embracing who you are honestly, rather than criticism and self-hate.

Now look at your list and accept that you are a mix of both. Get familiar with your "bad" side so it no longer controls you unawares. Draw on your "good" side so you're always getting the most out of your potential. From this list, you can start to get an idea of your needs, and these can begin to inform your authentic desires.

Can you use your list to inspire some new goals, or help you improve the goals you've already set for yourself?

The Stages of Change Model is something that can help you organize your efforts to motivate new change for yourself. Change is hard! It takes effort and energy. It's a process that takes time.

The first stage is **pre-contemplation**. For example, you may be aware that your hoarding behavior causes some problems in your life, but you're not fully aware of the issue yet and make no plans to change. Think of this as the denial stage. Neither are you fully cognizant of the issue, nor of the extent of its negative consequences. Here it's common for people to be occupied by the cons of changing rather than the advantages of doing so. To move to the next stage, ask yourself questions like: "Has this behavior seemed like a problem in the past too?"; "What would have to happen for me to change this behavior, and has that happened already?"; etc.

In the **contemplation** stage, you start to become aware of the problems with staying as you are, but are unsure about whether to change. Both the costs of changing as well as the need to do so start becoming more prominent. You might still be exploring possibilities, but lack confidence to do one thing: make the decision that the negative outweighs the positive, and so you need to alter your behavior. Your partner threatens to leave, and you realize something's got to change. In the absence of an external motivator, you might well be stuck in this stage for months and even years. To move past this, ask yourself if you see change as a process of giving something up rather than gaining something beneficial. Ask yourself what exactly is preventing you from transforming, and what you can do about those reasons or factors.

In the **preparation** stage, you start to investigate ways to change your behavior. You may seek out a therapist specializing in hoarding behavior, or consider hiring a cleaner. You're building confidence, commitment and intention, although nothing has yet actually changed. It's in the **action** stage that new skills are developed, even if a little help is needed along the way. This is where the hard work of change begins, and can be a time full of enthusiasm. There are several things you can do to make these incremental changes permanent. Chart out your next steps meticulously, gather more information regarding ways to alter your behavior, and seek external reinforcements through support groups, counselors, friends, etc.

Maintenance kicks in after a few months, where the challenge is to sustain the new behaviors and keep on top of things. It's all about focus, self-control and perseverance to cement the new gains. Here, it's natural to still falter and make mistakes, but don't be too hard on yourself for this. Treat it as a minor setback and look to avoid similar mistakes in the future through better planning.

However, there is also a chance of **relapsing**. You might find yourself reverting to your original behaviors despite making all this progress, and the disappointment you feel might discourage you from going through this hard work all over again. Relapsing also points to some flaw in the way you've proceeded through the previous stages. This could relate to your motivations, certain techniques you did or didn't use, etc. Take time to reflect on why you relapsed, and push yourself to come up with a better plan of action for round two.

If you manage to avoid relapse and the maintenance stage continues long enough, the **termination** stage is where new behaviors are fully integrated, and you're enjoying a new, improved life where relapse is the furthest thing from your mind. However, keep in mind that termination is rare, which is why this stage is often left out of health promotion programs. The urge to relapse usually remains in some form throughout. Use the benefits you experience from your new habits in the maintenance stage to combat such impulses whenever they arise.

Getting snagged at any stage comes down to motivation. This is why it's so important to work with your own biology, and to take the time to understand the *source* of your motivation, and whether or not it's actually working for you. To move your way over the long path that runs from where you are to where you want to be, you'll need plenty of support.

Find a mentor, a role model or someone who's done what you have to help you through those moments when you're close to giving up. Find someone who knows what it means to push against laziness and fear, and let their attitude rub off on you. Cut yourself some slack... It's not supposed to be easy. A healthy dose of self-empathy when it matters could keep you on course where self-judgment would only lead you to give up sooner and go straight back to square one.

If you're overwhelmed or unmotivated, scale down your sights to see only the single next step ahead of you. If even *that's* too big, break it down further. Take the next step, and don't worry about the one after that.

Remind yourself of your strengths, take a break if you need to, and tap back into your deep, intrinsic reasons. Picture yourself as you want to be—dedicated, strong, fulfilled, empowered. Hold on to this feeling and take heart that energy slumps or difficulties are par for the course, and won't last forever.

Troubleshooting Apathy

OK. Let's say you've done all that.

You've dug deep in to understand yourself, your needs, your strengths, your weaknesses. You've tweaked your environment, worked with your physiology, kick-started your dopamine and done plenty of self-examination. But you're *still* not motivated. What now?

Perhaps you're the person who starts each new project with hope and fire, but you fizzle out soon after. Perhaps you procrastinate so hard you never even start. Let's take a look at what can go wrong—and how to fix it.

Problem 1: You're not actually ready

Emotionally, cognitively, financially, practically—whatever the case, maybe you launched prematurely and now you're floundering. Change is a process. It takes time and planning. You can't leap to the action stage without having properly completed the contemplation stage. Fail to plan, plan to fail, as they say. Now, this isn't to say there's something wrong with not being ready. Recognize where you actually are in the process, and identify what you need to do next to move yourself along.

Problem 2: You dreamt too big

This is a theme you will see repeating throughout this book. "Reach for the stars" sounds nice, but grand, intimidating plans can actually feel paralyzing. Rather aim for baby steps and mini-habits. You can't do everything at once. You'll need help with some things, too—don't be a hero and do it all yourself.

You may need to organize your goals better, go back to the planning stage, and work hard to break those grand visions down into manageable, life-sized daily chunks. Just stick to your routine. Don't forget to soak up the dopamine-fueled sense of achievement each time you tick an item off the list!

Problem 3: You beat yourself up

So much motivational "self-help" out there is actually pretty harsh, when you think about it. By now, you can recognize punitive external motivators and motivation that just springs from insecurity and fear. Give yourself a little compassion, instead. It's OK for it to feel hard. It's OK to be on a learning curve, to make mistakes, to be scared, to miss a deadline, to change your mind. Importantly, *it's OK to rest*—you're not a machine.

Problem 4: You're overanalyzing

It's great to understand your deeper psychological motivations, or to thoroughly explore the pros and cons of a situation, or to try and be perfectly organized and prepared before you act. But eventually, you need to act. Often, you need to act even with incomplete information, and with some risk attached. That's OK! Sometimes, the only way to learn is to get in there and get messy.

Problem 5: You actually don't want what you think you do

In other words, it's not really your goal at all. Many people *think* they want an uber-healthy lifestyle and a ripped body, when they actually don't want to spend hours in the gym, give up alcohol and jog every single morning of their lives. Many people mistakenly think they want money and fame until they get it and realize they were actually chasing something entirely unrelated. If you're routinely uninspired by the goals you claim to want to achieve, it might be time to look closer at the claims themselves.

Problem 6: You have a resistant attitude

Feeling as though you "have to" do something is much like having an internal "overjustification effect"—it can drain your motivation entirely. But you are never forced. Reframe it to, "I choose to" because you *do* have the choice. Focus on your power to choose beneficial activities (even if they're sometimes difficult) and you'll feel more motivated. Stop telling yourself a story about how you can't do something, and just do it—new habits *will* take practice before they become more automatic.

Jump-start your motivation

Remember dopamine? Your brain's reward centers light up in the anticipation of a reward, driving your motivation and signaling to your brain, "Do it!" Work with this in-built process and you naturally improve your motivation. First, pay attention to what matters. Focus on the physical, emotional or social *benefits* of completing a certain action (not the difficulties or hard work). Take time to really visualize the reward and soak up those good feelings, to fuel your motivation processes.

Realize, also, that your willpower, energy and focus are finite—they do get depleted throughout the day. This is why a Columbia University study found that judges make more favorable rulings at the start of their sessions than later, when they're tired. Avoid "decision fatigue" by reserving your daily willpower for things that matter most.

Automate less important actions and make use of habit and routine to take decisions off your plate. Always start the day with the most essential task, and delegate or simply cancel activities that are unnecessary and only drain your energy.

When you're knee-deep in The Slog of working toward your goals, you need some lifelines to ensure you keep going. You can find enormous pockets of energy and motivation by constantly reconsidering your goals to make sure they actually align with your values, desires and needs. Remind yourself of why you're doing what you're doing, and visualize it fully—give your brain an image to work toward. When you feel calm and committed, it's so much easier to be resilient in the face of challenge or temptation.

Willpower matters—but it's your **values, vision and resilience** that make up that willpower!

Motivated people know how to make conscious choices guided by their values and skills. Ask yourself:

What choices have I made and what choices could I still make?

What are my strengths and weaknesses here?

What are my deepest values, needs and desires?

By answering these questions, you naturally strengthen and become aware of your *internal motivation*, and give yourself the chance to come into perfect alignment. When you act with clarity and awareness of who you are and what you want, you become unstoppable. You no longer need to find ways to be motivated. You already *are*.

Goals, Goals, Goals

Not all goals are created equal. To shape and direct your actions in the present, you need a goal to focus your efforts toward. A goal is a vision of the future that guides behavior in the present. A good way to formulate what you want to achieve is through the SMART mnemonic, which denotes five traits each goal must have.

A goal needs to be **specific** so you know exactly what you're aiming for. Saying you want to become a healthy individual is a vague goal. However, when you say you want to be someone who eats healthy, exercises regularly, and drinks enough water, that's a specific goal.

A goal needs to have some way of being **measured** and a form of feedback so you know how well you've done. One example is that you'll work out four times a week, or eat three healthy meals a day.

A goal needs to be appropriately challenging, but also **achievable**—not too easy or too hard or complex. You need to have the confidence and self-efficacy needed to actually complete it. Does your lifestyle permit you to work out and spend time preparing healthy food? Is this something you can keep up long-term?

A goal needs to be **relevant** to you— otherwise it's just an interesting possibility. Your aspirations are affected by your emotional state, needs and values. Unless these are activated, you won't fully commit to the goal. Ask yourself if becoming healthy is something you truly want for yourself or if you only want to look good for others.

Lastly, your goal needs to be **time-bound.** Set yourself a deadline for completing your goals. This subconsciously leads you to plan your goal and its achievement in ways that keep with your chosen target date. So if you want to bulk up, give yourself five months.

Remembering the role that dopamine plays, we need to take care in how we frame our goals. We need to *focus on the benefits* we expect, and frame outcomes in terms of positive rewards and not punishment or avoidance. What's more, we need to rank and prioritize a range of different goals that are fulfilled at different time scales. We can only do this effectively if we have a firm grasp of who we are, what the goal actually is, how to practically achieve it, and so on.

The quality of your goals impacts the level of your commitment and motivation. Your goals provide structure, focus and direction for your action, so once you've figured out the end goal (the "what"), you need to make sure you have a rock-solid plan to get there (the "how").

How to set goals the right way

You've now heard of SMART goals—goals that are Specific, Measurable, Attainable, Relevant and Timebound—and by now you can probably see *why* setting goals this way is so smart. Making a plan toward your goals needn't be complicated, but it does need to be done correctly.

Inspired by your vision and your values, you need to identify the **path** that leads from the present to the future, then make sure you have broken that path down into single steps. What could be more motivating than knowing you're on the road to get to where you want to be?

This applies to goals big and small, short-term or long-term, and in every area of life from relationships and career to artistic pursuits and education. Once you've got the bigger picture in place, it's easier to decide on the smaller tasks. You can complete these tasks with more enthusiasm when you know that they plug into the larger scheme. Your to-do list is then not a slave driver, but an exciting blueprint carrying you step by step to your dreams.

If you're unsure of which goals to prioritize, remember Maslow and revert back to your needs, asking which of your needs are more pressing than others. Write them all down (cap it at around twenty or twenty-five goals).

Next, circle the five goals that seem the most inspiring, interesting or urgent. Spend a moment to visualize each to feel out where you feel most naturally energized, and go with the goals that really fire you up. Go through each of the goals and ask yourself, what would life be like if I actually achieve these goals? What would change? Also ask what difficulties stand in your way and how hard it would be to accomplish this goal.

Use your answers and your gut feeling about each goal to select only those goals that will take your focus from now on. The rest can wait—don't allow them to distract you! Incidentally, Warren Buffett is said to use this technique. He felt it was better to have just five amazing but completely achieved goals than to chip away halfheartedly at dozens of more vague, unimportant ones.

Final tips for doing it right

A great hack for making sure you stick to your goals is to be specific—and this is *how* you can be specific:

When you frame an action on your to-do list, or commit to a habit, frame it in terms of *what, where, when, if, and then*. For example:

"Every weekday morning at 6:30 a.m. I am going to head to the gym to do a thirty-minute session before work. If I can't get to the gym, then I'll do my workout at home."

Be as specific as you can, because this will help you with the next tip, which is to follow the five-a-day rule. According to this, you must do five things, big or small, every single day that bring you closer to achieving your goal. This can be something as small as making a call or sending an email, but consistently doing five things a day and tracking these actions will fire up your dopamine receptors.

It may seem hard to believe, but researchers at the University of Bath found that people who framed their goals this way actually stuck to their goals better than those who didn't.

Another tip comes from the now famous book *It Works* by an anonymous millionaire: don't announce your goals until you've made some tangible gains toward them. Doing so too early usually strips your motivation because it gives you a premature sense of accomplishment and conclusion. As always, if you have to share, focus on processes and not outcomes ("I'm going to the gym on these days" rather than "I'm aiming to lose fifty pounds").

That said, there is one exception to this rule, and it's about accountability. Sharing with others can work if it creates a situation where there are real consequences for you in not following through. Having a close friend ask you every week about the progress you've made, for example, can be just the thing to keep you on track.

The Takeaway:

- Certain personality traits make motivation more likely—but you can encourage these traits in yourself. The OCEAN framework—openness, conscientiousness, extraversion, agreeableness, and neuroticism—is a good way to know whether you're the kind of person who is generally able to motivate themselves.

- One of the most common reasons we are unmotivated is because we are pursuing someone else's goals. This is where considering whether your motivations are intrinsic or extrinsic can help. Ask yourself why you want to achieve your goal; is it for yourself, or for some external reason like praise, social approval, etc? Generally, intrinsic motivation is the one you'll want to cultivate, but extrinsic motivation has its place too. The latter is helpful for small, short-term tasks, but everything else requires the former in some measure.

- Change is hard—but if you understand that it's a process, you can take it step by step. There are six major steps to consider. These are pre-contemplation, contemplation, preparation, action, maintenance, and hopefully, termination. This process starts by you becoming aware of some error in your ways and slowly realizing the need for change before you start taking concrete steps in that direction. Once you've done so, your new habits become increasingly ingrained, and ultimately permanent.

- If you've done everything suggested so far and yet are unable to motivate yourself, there are still some things you can do. Troubleshoot low motivation by tapping into your values, needs, weaknesses and strengths. Ask yourself questions like whether you're actually ready for your goals, consider if they're manageable or overwhelming, and if you're overthinking them too much.
- The quality of your goals determines the quality of your motivation—so make good ones! Follow the SMART

framework and ensure your goals are specific, measurable, achievable, relevant, and time-bound.

Chapter 5: The Economy of Motivation

You have exactly one life to do everything that you'll ever do. Act accordingly.

- *Colin Wright*

Behaviors cost. Motivation takes time, energy and resources. You have resources, but they're not infinite. How are you going to use the resources and assets you do have to most effectively achieve your identified goal? It's simple: you need to "budget" both the costs and resources wisely.

Everyday practical ways to strengthen motivation

Motivation is a habit, plain and simple.

It's made of nothing more than the tiny choices and actions of every day, piled up together, bit by bit.

Reduce Your Costs

The more you take conscious control of the motivation process, the more you realize it's not a question of sheer force of willpower; rather, it's about setting your life up in a way that best supports your natural motivation.

Sustained effort comes from have challenging but realistic (SMART) goals that really matter to you, to which you can be properly committed. You need realistic ways to tackle the daily hard work that comes with the *process* of reaching your goals—and for that you need to receive and implement valuable feedback that tells you how to adjust and correct as you go.

Because a process is all it comes down to. Successful people have not found a magical way to be perfect, but instead have become *experts at the process of constant improvement.* When they lack the mastery or organization needed, they figure out how to learn it. They proactively look around them for fresh opportunities. And when setbacks happen, they're not surprised in the least—they expect them, and respond with doubled-down resilience.

Here's a checklist to see whether you have all the necessary building blocks in place for genuine change:

- Mentors or people to guide and support you.

- A positive, intrinsically motivated mindset that focuses on your achievements already earned, as well as the benefits that will come with future goals.

- An honest awareness of your strengths, weaknesses, values and needs.

- A healthy lifestyle to support the physiological basis of motivation, and an environment that supports you rather than undermines you. You need plenty of ways to build and sustain energy every day.

- Dopamine! (Celebrate all those measurable mini-goals and dwell on the expectation of future rewards.)

- Self-compassion, and a respect for your gut feelings. An appreciation for who you are and the willingness to forgive mistakes and learn from them.

- A proper appraisal of associated risks and costs.

- A plan that breaks it all down realistically.

- Gratitude. Generate positive feelings by appreciating what you already have. Make positive, solution-focused thinking a habit and engage all the opportunities and relationships around you to ignite your motivation.

And even if you have *all of this*, the truth is that it still means very little unless one key ingredient is also in place:

HARD WORK.

That's it. This wouldn't be much of a book if it only contained those two words, but this honestly is the gist of it. No matter the planning and groundwork, and all the good intentions in the world, *nothing* happens until you put the work in.

Here's a little secret: sometimes, reading about motivation, making a plan to boost it, organizing your priorities, setting up the correct conditions, etc., etc., is simply a very sophisticated way to avoid doing the work. Resistance happens. Constantly. We need to act despite it. Constantly.

You could wait around for resistance to dissipate by itself, or you could spend some time trying to analyze and categorize it. You could dawdle with preparations and planning. But the truth is, change only happens at that boundary when you face down the fear and resistance...and push through it. Nothing else before that really matters.

Every day we are faced with a choice: take action that will grow our resolve and mastery, or avoid it and succumb to resistance, and feel bad about ourselves for having wasted the opportunity.

It may seem like an easy choice to shirk hard work today, but that's because the true cost only materializes later—when you feel aimless, unfulfilled and unchallenged in life.

Luckily, you have endless tools at your disposal to help with the more difficult parts of your journey. When facing down resistance, don't freak out. You missed a workout? You're suddenly feeling completely uninspired by goals you were crazy about yesterday? That's OK. It's human.

Go for a jog or check to see if any of your physical needs are going unmet. Head back to the drawing board to determine if your goals need tweaking. Or maybe it's your attitude that needs a boost? If you've been in grueling hard work mode, you may find your energy levels slumping until you can take time out to make a list of all you're grateful for, or remind yourself of the awesome qualities you possess to help you overcome your challenges.

Take a moment to reconnect to your deeper needs and visualize how your goal will satisfy those. If all else fails, just push yourself to do five minutes of your activity, and call it a day. Not every moment of the journey is going to be pretty!

As long as you've done the deeper work of understanding how your personal psychology and physiology feed into the motivation game, you're at liberty to play around with the almost endless number of hacks and tricks available to get you through the hard work.

Use productivity apps, seek out a study group or ask for help. Make a chart of all the progress you've already accumulated and internalize the fact that you are mid-process, continuing that trajectory right now, today. It might seem cheesy, but why not stick some quotes or inspirational images above your desk?

Remember that you're not the first to have to work hard this way, and that even the world's overachievers struggled just as you're struggling now.

Real Talk

We're now firmly in the territory most people have in mind when they think of motivational self-help material. The realm of "positive thinking" and the like. The difference is, you'll be able to undertake a lot of this advice armed with a richer understanding of *all* the aspects that go into creating motivation.

Let's look at positive self-talk in a more realistic way. Positive self-talk goes way beyond fluffy affirmations that seem a little out of touch with reality. Positive self-talk actually kicks in when things are their worst. When you're having a bad day, when nothing is going right and you feel stupid, or tired, or weak, or irritable. You look at yourself and your goal and feel like crap, and just don't want to do it anymore.

Then is the time to use positive self-talk.

Positive self-talk is a powerful tool to help you grind through (inevitable) discomfort. Ironically, it's acceptance of the fact that *yes, this is hard* that makes us stronger. We don't have to lie to ourselves.

"I've had a difficult morning, but that's OK. I'm still going to finish what I started."

"Hard work makes me stronger. I'm going to be stronger next time."

"Shit happens. I'm bigger than this. My life goals are more important than my temporary discomfort."

Discomfort can turn you down the other path—the path of complaining. This is where you deliberately teach your brain to focus on the negative and amplify it. Sounds great, right? You're immediately pulled away from focusing on the benefits, and suddenly all you can see is a million reasons *not* to carry on.

Moaning and whining without taking action only disempowers you (and makes you a pain in the ass to be around). Remember that you only have finite amounts of time, of energy, of focus. Why fritter it away on petty complaints about trifles that ultimately don't matter? Especially when that energy could be put toward something that does matter—i.e., being the person who *does* something to make the world better, rather than just sit around and complain about it.

Tempering optimism with realism

There is an old Sufi proverb that states, "Trust in God; tether your camel."

We all know someone who has vast, unexplainable stores of unrealistic optimism for life. They buy a lottery ticket and swear they'll win this time, or they're sure that the stage four cancer they've been diagnosed with can't hurt them if only they muster enough optimism to beat it. The truth is, unbridled optimism is as useless as unbridled pessimism, and just as unrealistic.

All human beings need hope and a sense of possibility in the future, but this should never stop you from taking an honest look at the material facts of the present, right now. This can be a delicate balance to strike. "Positivity" can, in a weird way, act in exactly the opposite way it's intended, making us less resilient and more prone to giving up.

As Kahneman of the now famous *Thinking Fast and Slow* explained, a little optimism can be an extremely useful bias to have, and can make us feel good about ourselves, our abilities and our prospects. But when you're trying to make concrete improvements, you may need to draw on a less popular teacher—**productive pessimism.**

Your slightly rose-tinted glasses do come in handy, but sometimes you need a cold hard look at reality—especially if the costs of being over-optimistic are high. When you're dealing with matters of life and death, with the law, with your health or with decisions that could cost you a lot of money, it's better to err on the side of pessimism.

Here, "productive" pessimism means learning to think with cold, hard rationality that actually results in benefits for you. Try this: Pick one of your goals and now, assume the worst.

Imagine that you've failed spectacularly. Conduct a "pre-postmortem" and ask, why did it fail? By exploring what went wrong, you uncover some of the potentially hazardous pitfalls you might have actually missed by being too positive.

For example, say you wanted to become a healthy person. But instead you've ended up gaining instead of losing weight while having spent a lot of money on your gym membership. Your energy levels have dropped due to improper nutrition, and all the time you wasted could've been spent productively elsewhere. How could this have happened? Maybe your workout routine wasn't rigorous enough, and you replaced unhealthy foods with other unhealthy foods.

Take what actions you can to minimize these potential risks. Then act. Re-engage your optimism by hoping for the best outcome, considering that you've done what you can. Trust in God—but don't forget to tether your camel, too.

So much of what's written about motivation is "positive"—all fist-bumps and trophies.

But truthfully, the real story is in all the boring stuff—the effort and slog and grind you undertake day after day, even when you're tired or unhappy. Some people ask, "What do you care about most? What do you love more than anything in this world?" as a way to uncover motivations. But it may be more helpful to ask, "What pain are you willing to endure?"

This is what it comes down to—not how big a goal you can concoct, but how much discomfort, pain and uncertainty you're willing to endure to achieve that goal. In the trenches, your willingness to endure and persist is infinitely more valuable than how inspired you can get when thinking about the rewards waiting at the end of the rainbow.

So, you're utterly exhausted. You don't want to work today. What now?

Here's a secret: It doesn't matter.

It may seem weird that a book about motivation is telling you that motivation doesn't matter, but consider this: your level of enthusiasm is not going to be 100 percent all the time. The biggest misconception that fuels procrastination cycles is that you can only achieve your dreams if you're firing away on all cylinders, all the time.

But people get tired. If you get tired, and you avoid your work, you feel anxiety, and this anxiety makes you procrastinate even more. How do you break the cycle? Just keep going. It's OK if you slow down a little, or are not quite at top notch—just keep an **unbroken chain** going, and your energy will pick up eventually.

Take just one step and feed off the momentum. Then take another. Whatever you do, don't dwell on the anxiety of putting things off. You'll find that even taking the tiniest step toward your goal releases that tension and gets you moving in the right direction again. Author of *The Motivation Myth* Jeff Haden believes that **feeling highly motivated is not a cause of action, but actually a result.** In other words—the fire to keep going often only pitches up long after you've taken those first sluggish steps!

Taking that first step can be hard if you think of your goals as duties and obligations, rather than something that is inspiring your growth and improvement. Break things down into smaller goals if necessary, and pace yourself. Once you tick one off the list, celebrate it—those good vibes power up the next step. While you're at it, commit to disregarding all those things that are nagging for your attention but which really don't matter. Delegate or postpone them.

Procrastination and feeling "lazy" is one thing, but what if you're genuinely burnt out and so stressed you can't get going? Stress and pressure can destroy your focus and sap the joy out of everything, no doubt. Firstly, you need to identify why you're stressed and how it's affecting you. Are you worried about deadlines or running out of time?

Next, give yourself permission to take a break and recharge, especially if you're feeling burnt out after prolonged stress. Don't confuse constant action with progress—you may get more done by resting appropriately than by killing yourself trying to be constantly in motion. Reach out to ask for help or inspiration from a peer. Pause and notice how far you've actually come. Have you even celebrated all those important milestones?

Pressure and hard work are par for the course, but take it too far and your body may forcefully tell you it's time to take a step back and recalibrate. Are your physiological needs taken care of? Have you strayed from your original passion or gotten sidetracked? Sometimes, you just need to simplify things so you can focus on what really matters. Clear the plate and look at the situation honestly. If you're consistently unmotivated by what you're doing, it could be that your passions have simply changed over time. Can you find where that sense of excitement has moved to?

If you're sure that you're still on the right path but just feeling depleted energy-wise, then there are a few hacks and tricks to get through the grind without losing too much momentum. Firstly, do the task that's weighing you down the most, first. Get it off your back, or at the very least, break it down into chunks and make some headway with one mini-goal.

Naturally, you need to reconsider your overall lifestyle to make sure you're giving your body what it needs. Grab a healthy snack, meditate for five minutes, go for a walk, do some stretches, take a nap or have a mood-boosting chat with a friend to refresh you.

Another good short-term fix is just to switch things up a bit. Bring in some fresh energy by moving to a different location than usual, or playing some upbeat music that always gets you feeling awesome. The same old same old can be uninspiring after a while—try do things a little differently and you may notice you weren't exhausted, just a bit bored.

If you're throwing everything you can at a stubborn feeling of exhaustion, then the solution is simple: you're burnt out and need rest.

Think "Least Effort"

Earlier, we used the word "lazy."

But being lazy can be a good thing—if we define lazy as wanting to find smart ways to do the least possible to get the most reward.

The principle of least effort says that, **all things being equal, a person will rationally choose the option that takes the least effort**. Though this may seem obvious to absolutely everyone, psychologists in the early '30s and '40s (primarily Clark Hull) were newly interested in applying certain economic principles to human behavior, and how our choices could be explained in terms of investment, costs, profits, supply and demand, and so on.

The idea is that our choices are consciously or unconsciously driven by a weighing up of how much a choice costs us, what's it's really worth, the benefits we acquire, the risks, and the quality of our other options. Whether you agree with this vision of human beings as purely mechanical, economizing entities or not, it's probably fair to say that the smart choice is often the one that results in the least expended effort.

What this tells us about motivation is that the impulse we call "laziness" is often just a natural human way of being frugal with energy and effort. That we strive to choose the "path of least resistance" is something we can work with, rather than against.

Taking it further, many Eastern philosophical traditions have more deeply covered this same topic in noting, as Lao Tzu did, that "nature does not hurry, yet everything is accomplished." Rather than this being purely a behavioral tendency, some have suggested it's nature/reality itself that follows the principle of least action, total ease, and harmony. Animals, plants, the ocean, the earth itself—none of it *tries* to do anything, it just does it by virtue of its own nature. Hence, there is no need for motivation. All we need do is move according to our own nature.

So, what is the right path?

Does the way to a fruitful, happy and healthy life necessitate endless time-management apps, goal-setting, TED talks, blood, sweat, tears, good habits that are endlessly, *endlessly* optimized, smart journaling, motivation hacking, overanalyzing, expensive supplements, "productivity porn," bizarre sleep schedules, quotes from American billionaires shared on LinkedIn…

…or is the path really about checking out of the rat race and pursuing the Zen-like paradox of non-pursuit (presumably with a pay cut)?

Is "least resistance" just laziness and lack of ambition, or is it a spiritually pure and profound acceptance of the flow of reality in which we are ultimately defenseless?

As usual, the best path lies somewhere in between. Though it might sound like a tall order, the truly appealing goal is to develop new habits to such an extent that they become automatic and filled with ease. In other words, a state of mind where doing the right thing *is* effortless.

The two approaches are not as different as they first appear. By honoring our natural inclination to get what we want with the least effort and force, we can simplify our process:

Principle 1: The shortest distance between two points is a straight line. If you want to go from A to B, go the direct path (i.e., every extra or unnecessary step makes things more effortful and less effective). Practically, this means you *only* do those things that effectively bring you to your goal (hint: extensive planning does not).

Principle 2: Know *exactly* what you're aiming for. The clearer you see it, the easier it is to target. A laser is more powerful than a dull, diffuse light beam.

Principle 3: Focus not just your vision, but your energy and attention. The more you put both in one place, the more effective you are. Cut distractions and commit to the thing that matters most.

Notice a theme in the above? It's all about simplification. The more minimal, the more direct and effective. Look at your daily routines and behaviors like a machine—are there lots of complicated, moving parts? Or is your life set up to cleanly and swiftly support only those items you've identified as being priorities?

Bruce Lee tells us to "hack away at the inessential"—streamline your work process, dump distractions, addictions and time-wasting behavior, and cut to the chase. Part of this process is sometimes actively culling what you previously identified as a goal. Can you delegate, rethink or simplify instead?

Some of us are prone to overcomplicating things because we falsely think it helps. We buy too much kit, waste too much time setting up various tools, or throw away an afternoon trying to "optimize" something that would have only taken five minutes to do anyway. Cut out all distractions (including the ones promising to make you more productive!) and keep focusing on that straight, elegant line between you and your goal.

No willpower, no effort, and no "motivation"—is it possible? Yes. But you need to be willing to trust that small, consistent habits done in a daily flow are often far more effective than forceful, drastic actions.

Make a small goal and then go from there. In nature, even the most enormous and powerful things start tiny, and then grow. Do the same with the smallest habit you can comfortably stick to daily. Then grow.

You don't have to abruptly change your life; gently divert its trajectory by piggybacking new behaviors on old ones. You don't need to do anything more than what you're already doing. Why force anything when you already have habits? You simply need to slowly pair the ones you have with the ones you want. Do it slowly and seamlessly, and you expend very little effort.

It's all about riding life's natural flow using ripple effects and the momentum from gradual changes. As an example, someone could identify the bare bones of their goal—to finish a novel within three months. He decides to ditch *everything* that isn't working toward this goal—and that includes procrastinating by going to writers' workshops, wasting time on writing blogs and doing "research."

The only thing that matters? Actually writing. He sets a goal for 2000 words a day. He's specific about this—it has to be 2000 perfect, polished words done at his desk, first thing in the morning, excluding Sundays. Identifying this goal, he pours his energy into it and only it. With this focus, his motivation naturally seems to strengthen. He can more easily turn away from distractions and just get on with the most direct path.

The irony is that this method will actually result in *more achieved but with less work*. It just makes sense—you only have so much time, energy and willpower. Why not dedicate it solely to the single most important goal? **Simplicity is empowering—too much complexity can weaken and dissipate motivation.**

Here's the secret about all those people that magically get so much done without seeming to break a sweat. It's not that they know about any fancy motivational tips and techniques that you don't. Rather, they've figured out *how* to use these methods in the most productive and effort-effective way possible.

It's great to plan your day the night before. To put your running shoes next to your bed so you're ready to go first thing in the morning. It's great to focus on protein-rich meals, exercise, and regularly meditate or listen to some relaxing music to bring down cortisol levels. And it's a brilliant idea to use journals, notes and to-do lists to keep yourself organized.

Bu the fact is that none of these things *in themselves* will stoke motivation or keep you going. Rather, they are effective only when used in service of a clearly identified goal which you have committed your full and focused energy toward achieving. Then, they become tools for success. For someone attempting to achieve a poorly formulated goal that they unconsciously don't even want, no smartphone app or motivational pep talk will make an ounce of difference.

If you're procrastinating or unmotivated, it's time to start asking questions:

- What's stopping me from acting?
- What are the benefits of completing this action?
- What will it cost to not do this action?
- Why is the thing I need to do important for me?
- What do I need to do to get started on this task?
- Do I have everything I need to act?

Finally, one last trick to beat procrastination: if you really, really, really don't want to do it, don't.

But tell yourself, "Either I do this, or I do nothing." No internet, no TV, nothing. Either you'll have a nice, much-needed rest, or you'll get so bored you'll do the task. It's a win-win.

Finally, let's consider one more factor to boosting motivation that is not often considered: the fact that motivation and enthusiasm are often *contagious*.

No man is an island. And yet when it comes to getting something important done, the assumption is often that we're entirely on our own and it's down to us and our singular willpowers to make it happen. In contrast to this perspective, a 2012 study published in the *Journal of Personality and Social Psychology* by Walton and colleagues suggested that belonging to a group can be powerfully motivating.

If you're thinking that beneficial social connections have to be made with mentors in your field, think again—*any* social connection proved effective, although obviously engaging with an expert has its perks. Humans are social creatures. We inadvertently take on the goals of others around us—a good or bad thing depending on how aware you are of the process, and how you use it to your advantage.

We all want to belong somewhere. It's a strong human need that we can't overlook when considering where our motivation comes from. Belonging to a group gives us a sense of identity, of security, of orderliness in the world...and, it turns out, it can shape and direct our motivations and behaviors.

"Motivational synchronicity" in workplaces rests on this ability to mirror and bond with others. Knowing that we are inevitably influenced by the motivations and goal-seeking behavior of those around us, it pays to **give some attention to who you surround yourself with**. Move toward those whom you admire, and a little of their motivation will likely rub off on you!

Interesting research has also suggested that the under-performance of your peers can measurably diminish your own performance. It's fascinating, when you think about it—when you behave a certain way, you are not just affecting your own outcomes, but those of every other person in the group, at the same time as they are affecting you.

Think of it this way—the positivity and enthusiasm you send out will likely come back to you. Your peer group matters, in both directions, and *everyone* in that group matters. Are the people you spend your time with inspiring you or subtly bringing you down? Or, seen in another way, are you missing out on opportunities to inspire and motivate those around you with your own behavior?

The Takeaway:

- Your resources are limited—consider the costs and rewards before you act, including the cost of *not* acting. However, once you realize you have everything you need to achieve your goals, you need to start the hard part: working toward them. Nothing can substitute for hard work, and ultimately that is the biggest factor in our success.

- As you put in the work, realize that positive self-talk and gratitude support motivation, while complaining kills it dead. You don't need to tell yourself positive platitudes that are out of touch with reality. Instead, if you're facing difficulties, acknowledge the position you find yourself in and encourage yourself to get past it.
- Learn to temper positivity with realism. Be a shrewd optimist—i.e., don't let your positivity be blind and inconsiderate of realities. Use productive pessimism to channel "negativity" in a smart way. We're constantly told to be positive, yet taking a cold, hard look at reality can often be truly beneficial. As you learn to balance the two, it's natural to make mistakes. Treat them as minor setbacks and move on.
- Choose the path of least resistance— use clarity of vision and focus to take the most direct path to where you

want to be. Laziness can sometimes be a boon, and if there is an easy way to do something, choose that every single time. While taking the harder path might feel more valiant, it isn't necessarily the more productive one. More work does not equal more results. If you can achieve your outcome through less effort, it's only rational to take that route instead, and preserve your energy for future endeavors.

- Most importantly: **motivation is not a cause of action, but its result.** Don't wait for motivation to come to you; actively seek it by putting in the hard work, day in and day out.

Summary Guide

CHAPTER 1: UNDERSTANDING MOTIVATION

- Motivation is the collection of psychological forces that allow us to **initiate, organize and persist** with behaviors that will ultimately lead us to the achievement of a goal. There are several ways to conceptualize what motivates us, but these can broadly be characterized into intrinsic and extrinsic motivators. Intrinsic motivators derive from our own desires and needs, as we feel an inner desire to accomplish certain goals, while extrinsic motivators come from external sources.

- Motivation is distinct from related concepts like happiness and inspiration. One can be happy but not motivated, and vice versa. The impulse that makes you do something isn't the same as the feeling of euphoria. Similarly, inspiration itself can be a motivator, but while inspiration is short-lived and unpredictable, motivation needs to be cultivated through discipline and action. Inspiration can also be a result of motivation instead of the other way round.

- Throughout history, different people have espoused different reasons and goals behind our motivations, and these have all culminated in the modern understanding of the concept. Aristotle was the first to recognize that motivation results from internal cognitive processes, while those like Locke and Hobbes recognized our desire for a particular consequence as what motivates us. Freud ventured into the subconscious territory of our brain to postulate that hidden sexual desires are behind our motivations. Today, frameworks like Maslow's Hierarchy of Needs dominate our understanding of motivation.

- Though motivation is a complicated concept, the reason it's so important is that we have finite resources for achieving our goals. By harnessing our power for motivation, we can be more resilient, more productive, and more goal-oriented in an effort to get what we want and incorporate the habits we desire. No goal has ever been achieved without motivation, and if you have large, long-term goals, motivating yourself is the only way to pull them off.

CHAPTER 2: THE SCIENCE OF MOTIVATED ACTION

- There are three main theories of motivation: instinct theory, drives and needs theory, and personal arousal theory. We can use our newfound knowledge of all three to guide our actions.

- According to instinct theory, our actions and behaviors are governed by universal impulses deep within our psyche. We exhibit these behaviors without being taught to, and all animals express them in similar ways. There are different ideas of what exactly an instinct is, but generally they are considered biological urges that serve a particular purpose and help us survive and thrive in the world.

- The drives and needs theory is similar in that it claims our behaviors are motivated by certain needs, such as hunger. However, while we have instincts to do particular things, our needs give rise to certain drives that aim to fulfill our needs. Maslow's Hierarchy of Needs effectively summarizes the various needs a person has throughout his life and which ones are more important than others. While this stratification of importance varies between people, Maslow's pyramid is a good way to recognize our needs, and thus working toward fulfilling them.

- Arousal theory claims that we all have an optimal level of arousal, also called homeostasis. This arousal can stem from a variety of emotions such as happiness, stress, anger, satisfaction, etc. All of our behaviors are aimed at achieving or maintaining this optimal level. While too little arousal is obviously bad, too much can be harmful as well because both inhibit our performance and motivation levels.

- We can use all three theories together to maximize our own motivation: trust your gut feeling but temper it with more rational thought; consider your needs when dealing with yourself and others; make sure that you're hitting the Goldilocks zone where arousal is concerned— not too little, not too much. As you utilize all three frameworks, remember to constantly break down large tasks into smaller parts, get enough rest, and to take breaks when you feel overwhelmed.

CHAPTER 3: HACK YOUR BRAIN AND BODY

- Evolutionary theory has taught us that most of our behaviors have come about because they ensure that we survive with changing times. Yet these natural endowments from nature are complimented by individual traits that make us unique. We can use this dichotomy to motivate ourselves by realizing where our strengths and weaknesses lie and developing them accordingly.
- Motivation can be seen as an ebbing and flowing state of arousal that expresses itself through thoughts, emotions, and behavior. To incorporate these disparate elements of motivation, Sung Il-Kim has suggested a tripartite framework that can help us utilize each of these components of motivation. According to this framework, there are three parts to cultivating motivation: generating it, sustaining it, and regulating it. By following this trajectory, we fire up the relevant parts of our brain that motivate us, which has a corresponding

physiological effect that arouses us into action.

- Three factors play a large role in helping you generate, sustain, and regulate motivation. These are your dopamine levels, circadian rhythm, and exercise.

- Dopamine is a neurotransmitter that plays a central role in the reward system of your brain. When you receive a reward for doing something, your brain releases dopamine and sets up a feedback loop which expects similar rewards in the future. By supplying yourself with rewards for completing goals and tasks, you can hack your internal reward system to motivate yourself.

- Your circadian rhythm is your internal body clock which determines the hours of the day where you're most active and attentive, when you feel sluggish, and when is the right time for you to rest. Some of us like to rise early, while others prefer sleeping in. Shape your routine according to your preferences for maximum productivity.

- Lastly, exercise is also an invaluable way to improve your concentration and increase serotonin. This has a tremendous impact on motivation levels, so make sure you exercise at least moderately several times each week.

CHAPTER 4: THE MINDSET FOR MOTIVATION

- Certain personality traits make motivation more likely—but you can encourage these traits in yourself. The OCEAN framework—openness, conscientiousness, extraversion, agreeableness, and neuroticism—is a good way to know whether you're the kind of person who is generally able to motivate themselves.
- One of the most common reasons we are unmotivated is because we are pursuing someone else's goals. This is where considering whether your motivations are intrinsic or extrinsic can help. Ask yourself why you want

to achieve your goal; is it for yourself, or for some external reason like praise, social approval, etc? Generally, intrinsic motivation is the one you'll want to cultivate, but extrinsic motivation has its place too. The latter is helpful for small, short-term tasks, but everything else requires the former in some measure.

- Change is hard—but if you understand that it's a process, you can take it step by step. There are six major steps to consider. These are pre-contemplation, contemplation, preparation, action, maintenance, and hopefully, termination. This process starts by you becoming aware of some error in your ways and slowly realizing the need for change before you start taking concrete steps in that direction. Once you've done so, your new habits become increasingly ingrained, and ultimately permanent.

- If you've done everything suggested so far and yet are unable to motivate yourself, there are still some things you can do. Troubleshoot low motivation by tapping into your values, needs, weaknesses and strengths. Ask yourself questions like whether you're actually ready for your goals, consider if they're manageable or overwhelming, and if you're overthinking them too much.

- The quality of your goals determines the quality of your motivation—so make good ones! Follow the SMART framework and ensure your goals are specific, measurable, achievable, relevant, and time-bound.

CHAPTER 5: THE ECONOMY OF MOTIVATION

- Your resources are limited—consider the costs and rewards before you act, including the cost of *not* acting. However, once you realize you have everything you need to achieve your goals, you need to start the hard part: working toward them. Nothing can substitute for hard work, and ultimately that is the biggest factor in our success.

- As you put in the work, realize that positive self-talk and gratitude support motivation, while complaining kills it dead. You don't need to tell yourself positive platitudes that are out of touch with reality. Instead, if you're facing difficulties, acknowledge the position you find yourself in and encourage yourself to get past it.

- Learn to temper positivity with realism. Be a shrewd optimist—i.e., don't let your positivity be blind and inconsiderate of realities. Use productive pessimism to channel "negativity" in a smart way. We're constantly told to be positive, yet taking a cold, hard look at reality can often be truly beneficial. As you learn to balance the two, it's natural to make mistakes. Treat them as minor setbacks and move on.

- Choose the path of least resistance— use clarity of vision and focus to take the most direct path to where you want to be. Laziness can sometimes be a boon, and if there is an easy way to do something, choose that every single time. While taking the harder path might feel more valiant, it isn't necessarily the more productive one. More work does not equal more results. If you can achieve your outcome through less effort, it's only rational to take that route instead, and preserve your energy for future endeavors.

- Most importantly: **motivation is not a cause of action, but its result.** Don't wait for motivation to come to you; actively seek it by putting in the hard work, day in and day out.

Made in the USA
Columbia, SC
01 December 2020

25967095R00111